TRUMPROPHECY

The Stone Cut From The Mountain Without Hands

By: Don Rohrer

COMING SOON

TRUMPROPHECY II - Healing America

Dedication

To critical thinkers. All over the world. Who feel increasingly isolated, alienated and alone. Who almost feel at times that liberty of conscience is just too big a price to pay in a world suffocating and dying from manipulation, control and group think. Who are made to feel immoral under the censure and wrath of religious and political tyrants, a staged media and twitter storm. The only immorality is the violation of your own judgments. You are not alone. I am not alone. We now have a president who is calling out the liars.

TRUMPROPHECY

Geo-political history and bible prophecy have just become one. A student of both
for many years I knew they must at some point merge. Looking in hindsight we can
now see they were in fact never separate. Prophecy is history. His-story. God's. He
rules in the affairs of men and nations.

The breakthrough for me came in understanding that the law is prophetic in that
men and events of our time were in fact written in code in the law and prophets, the
Covenant, some 3,000 years ago. In the sub-text of the Covenant, they were discovered and scientifically demonstrated to the world. Two international bestsellers, Bible
Code I and II shocked both the scientific and religious worlds. The problem is the dis-
covery itself falls short of revealing its true significance. Why did God allow mankind to
see individuals and events of our time in the law and prophets, proving scientifically the
text was inspired, came from outside man and time, at this moment of history? The dis-
covery was like finding the Ark Of The Covenant. It was however left to us to open it.

TRUMPROPHECY opens the Ark Of The Covenant. It unseals the ancient
prophecy of Daniel. It opens the book. Lets first of all understand why. In all that has
been written and taught on bible prophecy the church has utterly failed to deliver the nations, let alone deliver the truth. Like the media delivers fake news based on a false
narrative, the church delivers fake teachings based on a totally concocted school of
prophecy called "Futurism" itself based on a false Revelation.

There are only two pillars of truth that prophecy stands on. Remembering the
Law of Moses, and seeing Elijah appear. The law. And the prophets. I am not a Jew. I
am not a Muslim. I am not a Christian. I am, if anything, an Old Testament man of God.
So is Donald Trump. There is no Jewish God, no Muslim God, no Christian God.
There is only one God. And the truth of prophecy has absolutely nothing to do with religion. Religion is a man issued license to kill those who don't "believe". Wars don't
come from people. They come to them. They are imposed on them by those who exploit religious hatred for power and wealth. People like Bush and Clinton. Thats why
God brought Trump. Thats why all hell has broken loose. But I'm getting a bit ahead of
the story.

Remember when Moses came down off the mountain? What happened? He
held up the law and it split the nation wide open. Remember Trump promising to be the
"law and order" candidate? Remember his endorsement by law enforcement? Remember his pledge to honor those who protect us? What has happened in the wake of
his election? Widespread anarchy, chaos, rebellion, arson, mob violence, massive
demonstrations and lawlessness on many levels. Mayors, judges, cities and entire
states vowing to resist the president. In fact the entire nation has split into those sup-

porting the president, and those of "the resistance". There has even been an attempted mass political assassination and there is much talk of civil war. The nation has split wide open. This is the first and foremost indication Trump is, perhaps even unbeknownst to himself, the instrument of divine law. A stone cut from a mountain without hands is a picture of the law God put into the hands of Moses on engraved tables of stone. The mountain from which it was cut is the prophecy that determines all history. Daniel's prophecy tells us this stone, this law of God, will smash this final corrupt government, and pave the way for an entirely new and righteous government. By the time you finish listening to, or reading TRUMPROPHECY you can decide for yourself if God has put the power of divine law to fulfill history into the hands of Trump.

TRUMPROPHECY will review and explain clearly several prophecies and stories from the Covenant and apply them specifically to the rise of Donald Trump as our president. We will start with the oldest prophecy in the Covenant of God. These are words God spoke in the garden to the serpent which proclaim the liberation of mankind. We simply cannot understand evil in the world without identifying who is sitting in the seat of world power. A power Trump is facing on all sides.   Then we will fully explain the significance of Sept 11th as prophetically the beginning of "the end of days", followed by the Joseph Prophecy, showing why it foretells this day and hour and reaches to the 7th year of a Trump Presidency.   Finally, we will end with a stunning ancient prophecy of timing from Daniel, never before understood, which reaches to 2026, nine years from now, and just two years beyond the end of a Trump Presidency.

Before we get started we need to get some background to help us understand the powerful events we see playing out in this hour. We need to understand the context of our time. To do that we need to ask some questions. . .

Why has the rise and presidency of Donald J. Trump fueled what Trump himself has called "the greatest political witch hunt in the history of the United States"? Why has the political establishment, both Republican and Democrat, aligned itself in unity and solidarity with the mainstream media in a coordinated assault to bring down the president? Why has he been savaged by both liberals and conservatives?

Why did Trump rallies turn into spontaneous cries for justice with chants of "lock her up, lock her up"? Why did Trump call Hillary Clinton "the most corrupt person ever to seek the office of president of the United States"? Why, in the face of massive evidence of criminal wrongdoing, and obstruction of justice, do the Clintons appear untouchable and above the law? Why is Trump the first president to declare intentions of "draining the swamp" and actually taking steps in that direction? Why is scandal, corruption, waste and fraud gripping virtually every office of the Federal Government and no previous president has dared confront it? Why has Sean Hannity called Washington D.C. "sin city".

Why is Trump the first to speak to the people in their own language while virtually all his predecessors spoke a politically correct double speak designed to hide the truth?

Now lets consider the people. Why is Donald Trump causing media hysteria and massive and unprecedented civilian uprisings and demonstrations throughout the country on virtually everything he does and says?   Is it just that the democrats are sore losers, or is there something more to this? Why are pro-Trump individuals and groups being attacked and in many cases being denied their lst Amendment rights to free speech? Why are university administrators and presidents suddenly very active instruments in the hate Trump narrative and the only rules on campus, are rules for radicals? Why is fear and intimidation now sweeping the nation and anyone daring to support Trump openly called a bigot, racist, Nazi or worse?

Why are highly paid Trump haters in news and entertainment able to demonstrate beheadings, stabbings, shootings, and able to make other threats including blowing up the White House, when these acts constitute threats against the president for which any normal, obscure citizen would be investigated and prosecuted? Why are the famous Trump haters apparently exempt from prosecution?

Why has the hate Trump narrative now reached the point of a mass political assassination attempt which could easily have killed 15 or 20 Republican lawmakers? Why is the widespread anarchy, chaos, rioting, demonstrations, arson, property damage, injury, death, personal attacks and in fact the assassination of constitutional liberty and due process, all widely predicted by the left to occur should Trump lose, now the obvious strategy of the left, in the wake of a Trump win? Why is Hillary Clinton increasingly reappearing in "the resistance" to Trump?

Is the nation, in fact, on the brink of civil war? Why is the Bush family absolutely silent in all of this? What is the Bush-Clinton power, and who do they really work for? Why has Trump aroused this hidden power? Why must it destroy him? What does prophecy tell us about who Trump is really confronting, and how does it describe the final battle with this power?

Why is Trump pursuing "America First" policies? Is he just tapping a nationalistic populism, or is he actually working, perhaps unwittingly, to see America as the first nation into the Kingdom of God? Why is he seeking prosperity and wealth for the nation? Why did God give him the power to get wealth? Is it so we can all do well and have good jobs, or is there something deeper, much deeper? Why is he seeking to unlock America's natural resources, her true wealth, for the good of the people, instead of perpetrating corporate monopoly?

Is Donald J. Trump, in all that he is doing, actually advocating righteousness in government? His sudden appearance, and rise to the presidency is not an accident or even the result of his monumental devotion to the country. His drive, his hard work, his will, even his wealth to fuel his own candidacy did not bring him the presidency. Nor did we the people. It is because he is the one prophecy foretold who would come from the people, acting for the people. Speaking the language of the people. But it is even more. He is speaking the language of God. A language of ending corruption. A language of justice. At some point prophecy indicates he will actually call for national repentance and the formation of a new government. It is staggering to realize that the founders were guided by the God of history to call for a new government when the present government reached institutional failure. When corruption rules. When corrupt leaders become untouchable, and honest leaders are portrayed as corrupt. And the people suffer. That is where we are today. We will explain why this prophecy, written into the Declaration of Independence, is actually the same prophecy from Daniel written in constitutional language. It identifies the same corrupt power ruling then and now, it helps us understand who we are as a people, and perhaps most all, allows us to see the glorious destiny that awaits America.

Donald J. Trump is fulfilling multiple prophecies of the law and prophets. Collectively it is called "TRUMPROPHECY" and it explains virtually everything we are seeing unfold in this country today. TRUMPROPHECY will breakdown and explain multiple old testament prophecies making them plain, understandable and clear. It will answer all the questions. TRUMPROPHECY is a political and theological earthquake based on the only inspired text ever given to mankind, the law and prophets.

*   *   *   *   *   *   *

So lets begin by understanding something. It is a closely guarded secret but widely known fact that Donald Trump knows the truth of Sept 11th. That truth is the reason we have known $6Trillion worth of war for the past 16 years with no end in sight. Trump knows why the media pounds us every night with a "perpetual war" that will go on "for decades".

Remember the outrage and outcry during the campaign when Trump called George W. Bush a liar? Calling a former president and leader of the Republican party . . . . a liar? Remember that? Remember the weapons of mass destruction that did not exist? The pretext for going to war in Iraq? The start of the war on terror? Well, Trump told Wolf Blitzer of CNN: "The whole thing was a lie". Wolf pressed him, "What do you mean, the whole thing was a lie". Trump back peddled a bit . . . "There were no weapons of mass destruction". But looking back now we know there was much more to Trump's statement. What "whole thing" was a lie? Was Sept 11th itself . . . a lie? Was Trump saying that Sept 11th "the whole thing" was a lie? Why would he call George W. Bush a liar and then stand there so cool under fire from the media onslaught? He knew something. Its called the truth. In this case the truth of Sept 11th.

Donald Trump is a builder. He knows most of the top architects and construction engineers in the world. He knows perhaps as well as anyone in this world how a building is constructed and what it will withstand. Lets add what we know to what Trump knows. We know that no building, tower or skyscraper in the modern era has ever been knocked down by fire. It just doesn't happen because it can't happen. Witness the 27 story apartment building in London recently engulfed in fire on every floor. Every floor. Next day the charred remains. . . still standing. Go ahead, Google the subject. Start with "Planes without People". Go ahead. Then Google Transportation Secretary Mineta's sworn testimony to the 9-II Commission. Of how Vice President Cheney, in a bunker under the White House on Sept 11th, KNEW a plane was approaching D.C. airspace. Of how he maintained the order NOT to shoot down. You know, the one that hit the Pentagon. That one. Go ahead.

We also know no airplane has ever knocked down a building either. They can crash into buildings, but they don't knock them down. The intense steel grid that sheathed both the World Trade Center towers was designed, fabricated and tested to destroy an airplane. To withstand multiple airplane crashes from all directions at the same time. To withstand a hurricane. An airplane is a fragile aluminum shell that breaks apart on impact. And this doesn't even consider the core of the towers, the massive steel i-beam columns 4 inches thick and several feet across, that would not have been affected by fire or an airplane, but which literally vaporized in a matter of seconds during the collapse. What kind of energy could have vaporized the steel core? Turned them to dust?

So lets ask a question I bet you have never heard the media ask: Why would more than 3,000 architects and construction engineers sign a petition to re-open the investigation into the destruction of the World Trade Center towers? Why? Because they don't believe the government. Their own education, training, and construction experience totally contradicts the lie we have been told about Sept 11th. Here is another question I bet you haven't heard asked on the nightly news: How many of those architects and construction engineers do you think Trump knows? These are the biggest in the world. All of them? Most of them? I think you get the idea. And oh yeah, the 50 story WTC Tower #7 that fell down several hours later having never been hit with an airplane but "falling debris" and the resultant fire that had "weakened" it to the point it had to be "brought down" . . . well . . . the only problem with that is that it takes weeks and in some cases months to properly wire a massive tower for demolition. Did they wire it after lunch when it was supposedly on fire and weakened? They announced that WTC Tower #7 was going to be "brought down". Thats called a demolition. And why was WTC Tower # 7 totally vacated on Sept 11th anyway? Why? Do you think the fact it housed massive files on government and corporate corruption, that needed to be destroyed, could have been a reason? Give it some thought.

If we add all the eye witness testimony of hearing multiple explosions throughout WTC Towers One and Two, starting in the basements and lobbies, the bottom of the buildings, to the film footage showing the "squibs", multiple explosions bursting from the sides of the towers in descending sequence just ahead of the collapse, we are clearly witnessing a demolition. Virtually all the top demolition companies in the world have testified that although it appears some unconventional weapons or explosives, unfamiliar to civilian blasters may have been used, they all concur it was a demolition. In addition, aviation experts, including the man who developed the Lear Jet, have testified that the angles and trajectories of impact for the aircraft involved were impossible to achieve with jumbo jets. So what happened on Sept 11th, whatever it was, was not the hijacking of jumbo jets by Middle Eastern men with boxcutters under orders from Osama Bin Laden holed up in a cave in Afghanistan. It was something else. A conspiracy. A conspiracy to force a geo political outcome. To drive government policy in it's wake.

Did you know that the news media missed the big story of Sept 11th? How shocking. The big story is, it failed to tell the American people that George H.W. Bush was in a business meeting with the Bin Laden family in Saudi Arabia, discussing common oil interests, the day before Sept 11th! He and Osama Bin Laden go way back together. To the days H. W. "Poppy" Bush created and financed him through the CIA to help fight the Soviets in Afghanistan back in the 80's. Bush and Bin Laden were tight. Bush created him! Even so, I'm sure we can't imagine the shock Bin Laden must have felt when he realized he had been set up as the patsy for Sept 11th. That Bush family. You gotta watch 'em.   A bunch of real double crossers.

This is the truth Trump knows about Sept 11th. That it was a false flag "terror" event to open the back door to war in the Middle East. Under the George "W" "Bush Doctrine" of War On Terror, er. . . I mean "nation building" we could kill two birds with one stone. We could not only go after and kill all the terrorists for what they did to us on Sept 11th, but we could leave democracy, truth, justice and the American way in our wake. We will be welcomed as liberators! Bush and Clinton insiders will make a lot of money on the war. Its a win-win deal. And little Georgie can then get up in front of dinner crowds, you know White House journalists, and joke about looking for WMDs under the table cloth! None there. . . Don't see any under here. . . How funny! How absolutely hilarious! Boy those media people make a good crowd. They know a good joke when they hear it. Then for a cool $100K cash and a private jet Dubya will show up at fund raisers for wounded vets! This grotesque tragedy is the sad and devastating reality for many military families all over this nation.

And these families began to hear a different voice when Donald Trump spoke of the war on terror during the campaign. He spoke not of perpetual war, nor decades, nor even the "war of the 21st century" (a Bush favorite) no, he spoke of the massive humanitarian crisis gripping the Middle East and Europe. He spoke of the rise of Isis and the savagery the world has not seen since the Dark Ages. He spoke of $6Trillion dollars in American treasure that could have re-built America 2 or 3 times over. He spoke of taking care of our vets and honoring those who paid the ultimate price. He spoke of ending the war, using everything within America's power, knocking the hell out of this scourge Bush and Hillary Clinton had loosed on the world, and coming home! He spoke of ending war. He spoke of peace, what Churchill called "the most noble instinct of man". This was a different kind of man. He knows the truth of Sept 11th. The "whole thing" was a lie! This is why Trump is determined to end the war, and why the entire establishment is at war to bring him down. If Trump succeeds, the war will end, and the entire power structure in America will be dismantled. A massive tidal wave of indictments will follow. A day of reckoning. Justice at last. The prophecy of beast government being smashed by a stone cut from a mountain without hands, is being fulfilled before our very eyes!

This is where we begin to grasp the magnitude of TRUMPROPHECY. Institutional government corruption, the way of life for so many, will end. Their private jets. They massive financial rewards. Their political payoffs. Their protected estates. Their fawning media. Their influence. Their power. And thats what this is, the ultimate and final battle for power in the world. It is Lucifer's final assault on God's law, and the final attempt to bring the world into universal worship of himself under a one world government. That is what this is all about. This is for all the marbles.

Where did their corruption begin? Where did they begin? In the oldest prophecy in all the Old Testament. Eve had sex with Adam and had a son named Abel. She also had sex with Lucifer, the "serpent" and had a son named Cain. Not exactly the story of the apple and a talking snake, but none the less the truth. Forbidden fruit is always sex, not knowledge. Maybe the church can issue a story retraction. At any rate we all know that Cain killed Abel. There has been a lot of killing ever since. The reason this killing took place is that God said it would because Cain had a different nature than Abel. You see Cain was the "seed of the serpent", a conniving manipulator, a hunter, a predator, while Abel was the "seed of the woman" a person who would be led by his conscience, knowing right from wrong, and would always try to do the right thing. Two very different races of man would result. Actually, only one race is man. Abel is human. Cain is a humanoid-serpent hybrid. He looks human, but has a very different nature. He had a different father.

God said these two races of beings would have a perpetual "enmity" between them. Antagonism. Warfare. The "seed of the serpent" would afflict the "seed of the woman" throughout all of history. Bruise the heel of mankind. It started quickly with the death of Abel. But eventually the "seed of the woman" (mankind) would "crush" the "seed of the serpent". Cain's line of offspring, the serpents, would become world leaders and rulers. Abel's would become the "people", mankind. Yes, there are serpents among the people, and people among the serpents. The real enemy of people is not the so-called "Devil" or "Satan" or "Demons". The real enemy of people is serpents that look like people. Our warfare is not "spiritual". It is real. Drug traffickers, human traffickers, serial rapists, serial killers and the incorrigible wicked are real among us. Many are in the pulpits of religion. Their master is Lucifer, and they know and serve him as a real man. Abortionists are disciples of the pagan god Moloch. Child sacrifice is at the heart of their belief. Hillary Clinton, an abortionist, for example is a 6th degree Illuminati witch and slave handler. Most of her weekends during Bill Clinton's presidency were spent at a witch coven in LA. They all answer to their master Lucifer. The media won't touch this because it would expose them as accessories. The church won't teach this because it would unmask the real enemy of mankind, and false religion would come crashing to the ground.

The Lucifer-serpent-seed rulers, beginning with Nimrod at ancient Babylon, would rule the world throughout the beast empires that were to rise and fall over the course of world history until now. Babylon, Medo-Persia, Greece and finally Rome. These are the four empires the prophet Daniel saw in a dream. They would afflict the people in war and human trafficking. The last beast empire Daniel sees, Rome, is given to a flame and destroyed by fire. Fire is always the law of God in prophecy. Daniel also saw the same beast empires in the dream of King Nebuchadnezzar who built ancient Babylon into the first great world ruling empire. It was the head of gold of a towering image of a man in the king's dream. The king sees a stone cut from a mountain without hands strike the massive image in its feet which represent Rome the final world ruling empire. The stone destroys the entire towering image of a man, pulverizes it to dust. The stone than becomes a mountain filling the whole earth. Daniel's interpretation of the King's dream, the image of a man, and his own dream of the beast empires represent the same thing. The feet in the king's dream, and the final beast in Daniel's are represented by prophetic language describing the final installment of serpent ruled beast government. A final world ruling empire that is then destroyed by a stone smashing the image in the king's dream, and a beast given to a flame in Daniel's. So the fire in Daniel's dream and the stone in the king's dream represent the law of God emerging to destroy corrupt government worldwide.

The stone, the law, then becomes or orders a kingdom that will spread to all nations of the earth. The peace and increase of this kingdom, on earth, will know no end. It is the dawn of eternal justice and righteousness for all mankind. It is the dawn of righteous government that will include a resurfacing and re-configuration of the earth. The oceans will be greatly reduced opening vast new areas of rich fertile land and natural resources. Violent weather, flood and drought will end forever. God's true "climate change" will occur.   With this glorious new day will come a resurrection from the dead and immortality for those who inherit the kingdom. After that, in God's perfect time and order, repentance and immortality will be offered to all mankind. Past, present and future. The "seed of the serpent", the wicked, will be destroyed, left with neither "root nor branch", as if they had never existed. God even extends to them perfect justice with extinction. There is no "hell" or "hellfire". "Hell" is merely the grave where beings sleep until the resurrection and judgement. What a great and good father and God is our Creator to all people! His judgments are true and righteous. God is not willing that any are "left behind". That is a Lucifer inspired lie designed for terror and control of people. Father God has reserved many things unto himself, including apparently the ultimate fate of Lucifer.

So we are beginning to get a picture. At some point, prior to the resurrection, when corruption in government becomes truly global, we reach what prophecy calls "the end of days". We know that Sept 11th signaled to the world that "end of days" had begun. We know this. It was written into the sub-text of the law some 3,000 years ago. The law is prophetic, that is to say literally alive. It has been scientifically demonstrated to the world. It is not open to debate, controversy or opinion. Prophecy tells us when this happens, when "end of days" is reached, a man will come from among the people carrying with him the people's cry for justice. Justice is the precious fruit of the law.

When Trump emerged as the Republican nominee, he declared that Sept 11th "the whole thing", was a lie. He talked openly about government and media corruption. He called out the liars. When he did widespread awareness of Clinton corruption, global corruption, literally erupted all over the country. "Lock her up, lock her up" became the cry of the people, those who Clinton would label "deplorable". What no one realized at the time was that the nation would split wide open as a result of the cry for justice.

Again, the "stone" represents the law that eventually rises to destroy corrupt government. It seems hardly coincidence that a man named Roger "Stone" has been the foremost witness to Bush-Clinton corruption in recent years. His extensive writings, books and lectures are legendary. If he were slandering or libeling Bush-Clinton he would find himself in court being sued for millions. But a court of law is the last place a Bush or Clinton wants to go. Stone is a close advisor to Trump. Another man named Stone, Oliver Stone, produced and directed the JFK movie, you know the one, the "story that will not go away". While it definitely did not reveal JFK's killers, it proved beyond a doubt to a moral certainty, that Lee Harvey Oswald did not. We now have two men named "Stone" exposing corruption at the highest levels of world government. Coincidence? Not according to bible prophecy. This was predicted and written about 3,000 years ago.

Corruption has reached critical mass in our government with the Barak Obama puppet who was installed to pave the way for Hillary Clinton. His role was to transfer the last vestiges of democratic influence to the deep state by executive order. Hand her a dictatorship-in-waiting. His slow, cadenced, hypnotic delivery indicates he is under some form of mind control. The fact that he never delivered a single original thought, word, idea or program is the evidence. Nothing but slogans and mantras and more government via his health care law. You know, hope. . . change. . .tolerance . . .yes we can . . . diversity . . . and big brother. Wow, he is a monument to his masters. And his personal side is even darker. Go ahead. Do a few searches on his cocaine addicted homosexual history. The gay lovers he had murdered all within 6 weeks of each other during his rise to the Democratic Nomination in 2007. And his transgender wife Michael (Michelle) Robinson. Their kids are adopted. And how about his little slave girl, the Attorney General Loretta Lynch, the "linch-pin" in the Clinton-Obama corruption machine? A woman who told Comey to stand down on the FBI probe of Clinton. Not recommend probable cause. A woman who met with Bill Clinton privately just prior to Comey's capitulation to Clinton's pressure. A woman who stared down Comey assuring him the full wrath of the Clinton machine should he not cooperate. Comey knows full well how many dead bodies are in the wake of the Clintons. Comey, under threat, then leaks to the media for the express purpose of getting a Special Counsel appointed to investigate Trump, thereby getting himself off the hook with the Clintons and unleashing the frontal assault on Trump. Now he can write a book and make a few million since he is out of work and needs the money. Another political whore and his story of "service" to the nation.

So lets be real clear about what this means. About what is really happening. Comey's handiwork, the Special Counsel Robert Mueller, has unlimited discretion, power and budget. He answers to no one except his hidden masters. He is under orders to take Trump out. He will continue to "investigate" the so-called "Trump-Russia Collusion" false narrative until he is literally tearing the Trump Administration, Organization, and family, apart. At some point he will reach too far and Trump will fire him. In political terms its called a "Saturday Night Massacre". They have already goaded Trump into declaring a "red line". He didn't have to. The reality is Mueller, the Special Counsel will force Trump's hand to fire him, red line or not. When Trump fires him, or has someone else fire him at his direction, it will immediately trigger an "obstruction of justice" charge against the president. With that will come Articles of Impeachment from the House of Representatives. Its the law. An "obstruction of justice" charge meets the standard for impeachment. They now have Trump in a corner, and they can smell blood.

WARNING: If you are easily frightened or cannot stand the truth you need to stop reading right now. This is a legislative, judicial, media, and intelligence coup. The politicians in the congress will not dare stand with Trump. They will run for their political lives. After a sham trial in the Senate Trump will be impeached. If that happens there will be Civil War in the streets. An unprecedented civilian uprising in reaction to the coup in Washington. Half this country, the half Hillary called "deplorables" will react. This won't be like the last Civil War we had. This will be with drones, tanks, armored personal carriers and militarized police forces under orders to bring down Martial Law. Gun sales were at an historic all time high this last year, so people, millions all over the country, sense we are very near a powerful moment. Its now a matter of time, perhaps only a few months. If you have ever sought true repentance and the protection and provision of Psalm 91, then now is the time for you and your family. The Kingdom of God is coming soon whether Trump succeeds and God sustains him, or they take him out. The corruption is going to end. Along with the lives of the wicked. Donald Trump has already fulfilled TRUMPROPHECY whether they take him out or not. This needs to be understood. Trump is an instrument of divine law, just like with Moses. When Moses brought the law, the nation split wide open. Look familiar?

There are four elephants in the room:

lst - The Republicans, controlling both houses of Congress refuse to do anything but sit on their hands. The never were with Trump. Trump is a populist, a freedom fighter. The Republicans are politicians who refuse to move the president's agenda forward while refusing to go after the real criminals, starting with Hillary Clinton. They are colluding with the Democrats to let Trump beg and twist in the wind until he is taken out. Both parties are controlled by the same hidden power. Always have been. This is the legislative part of the coup. These politicians don't want to be on the wrong side of power after the coup.

2nd - The massive evidence of criminal wrong doing, and obstruction of justice relating to Clinton, Obama, Lynch, Comey, Rice, the DNC and others, is not even being raised as an issue! Not a whimper from the FBI, Justice Dept or the Intelligence or Judiciary oversight committees in both houses of Congress. The rank and file in the FBI, who did all the hard work to uncover massive Clinton corruption, have been totally betrayed. This is the legal, judicial part of the coup. The REAL corruption is being ignored.

3rd - The media false narrative-fake news of "Trump-Russia-Collusion" has been, from the beginning, the propaganda arm of the coup and the means to facilitate Comey's leak which allowed the naming of a Special Counsel, Bob Mueller. Once this happened it became only a matter of time. Mueller will force Trump to fire him. Attorney General Jeff Sessions was either compromised, somebody got to him, or he realized it was a no win situation and recused himself at the outset. When the Justice Dept lost control of the so-called "Russia" investigation, with Sessions stepping aside, the sharks could taste blood in the water.

4th - And finally, we come to the covert-intelligence aspect of this. It is critical to connect the dots in this drama. So lets do that. The collusion between the Clinton campaign and the DNC (Democratic National Committee) to deny Bernie Sanders the Democratic nomination, after he was used as cover for Clinton to move to the extreme left, was discovered and leaked to Wikileaks by a 27 year old DNC staffer named Seth Rich. Rich was a Sanders supporter greatly disillusioned by the Clinton-DNC treachery to defeat his candidate. He was gunned down on the streets of Washington D.C. by Bush-Clinton assassins on his way home one night from a bar during the first week of July 2016. The area had no previous history of violent crime. Obviously Clinton feared he might go further in public with what he knew. He was an eye witness. His testimony could have brought down Hillary Clinton.

Within 2 weeks of his death, on July 22nd, Wikileaks broke the story of the Clinton-DNC collusion to defeat Sanders. Seth Rich chose Wikileaks as a means to get it out there and remain anonymous. To avenge what Clinton had done to Sanders. Obviously he feared Clinton. The D.C. cops to this day call Rich's death a robbery, yet none of his personal possessions were missing. Nothing. Most notably his wallet and money. Obviously the D.C. cops feared Clinton as well, to close the case on such an obvious falsehood. Why was it classed a robbery? Nothing indicated it was a robbery. There has been absolutely no clue about the case to date. Nothing. No one, other than Hillary Clinton and Debbie Wasserman Schultz, the DNC Chairwoman, had a motive to kill Seth Rich. He was a universally liked young man with no prior history on anything. His brutal introduction to Clinton corruption cost him his life.

In the wake of the Seth Rich-Wikileaks disclosures, Debbie Wasserman Schultz resigned as head of the DNC, only to be hired by Hillary Clinton as her campaign manager. She had proven her loyalty. The Obama-Comey FBI and the Obama-Lynch Justice Depts attempted a feigned and phony "investigation" of the DNC based on the Wikileaks disclosures. They were told to go away. They did. The DNC refused to turn over anything. These are felony convictions for Obama, Comey and Lynch right out of the gate, and obstruction of justice for Donna Brazile, who had taken over for Schultz as head of the DNC. You know, the woman who would claim "christian persecution" for leaking talking points to CNN. Yeah, thats the one. All these rats came out of the same sewer.

Obama, Clinton and Schultz then planted the story with their co-conspirators in the media and intelligence communities, that Russia, not the DNC, was the source of the Wikileaks disclosures. That it was Russia that hacked into the DNC for the purpose of showing Clinton's dirty tricks, to throw the election to Trump! That Trump himself was in fact in collusion with the Russians! That the Russians and Trump were in a conspiracy to undermine our pure and sacred democracy itself! Oh, the self-righteous indignation of the far left who only want to preserve truth, justice and the American way! The floodgates to Russia-Gate were thrown open. The pre-coup was underway. It was now open season on Trump! In other words, caught red-handed and guilty, Clinton and Schlutz then project their own guilt on to Trump! Turn things totally upside down! Wikileaks has maintained all along that Russia was NOT their source for the DNC disclosures. They have never been proven wrong on any leak to date, and, they never compromise a source. Regardless of what you think of Wikileaks, these are the facts. Wikileaks is protecting Seth Rich's family with this integrity. Seth Rich's family, along with millions of other families around this nation, need to open their eyes.

Obama had laid the groundwork for all of this when, by Executive Order, he greatly expanded the network for intelligence sharing. The intent was to hand Hillary Clinton a police state after her victory. He handed her instead, after her loss, a network of Obama deep state operatives who then began a campaign of leaks to undermine and eventually bring down the Trump presidency. At least one major leak per day since Trump has been president. Clinton-Russian operatives, and others with vague connections to the Kremlin would then lure Trump people into all kinds of bogus meetings in the run up to the election to be used as "evidence" of collusion. An obvious and transparent sting operation. The drumbeat for impeachment began even before Trump was sworn into office.

We now have also learned that one Imran Awan, a former IT aide of Debbie Wasserman Schultz was arrested at Dulles International Airport on July 25th attempting to board an airplane. Awan has been the target of a U.S. Capital Police and FBI investigation that resulted in the capture of smashed hard drives and other computer equipment at his home just one day earlier. Perhaps he learned how to destroy computer evidence from Hillary. She seems to be an expert. So far he has been charged with bank fraud. He was also over-charging members of Congress for services, as well as engaging in blackmail attempts using member's emails and information he gained via his access to government servers. He and his brothers bilked the congress out of millions, while shipping hundreds of thousands out of the country. His brothers and family have already fled the country. While all other congressional members dropped Awan and his "services" many months ago, Debbie Wasserman Schultz kept him on her payroll until the day before he was arrested! Why? Debbie Wasserman Schultz is also apparently frantic over the seized computer material. Why? The mainstream media is ignoring this story. Why? Because it could all well prove that Hillary Clinton and her operatives, chief among them, Debbie Wasserman Schultz, were the originators of the Trump-Russian-Collusion conspiracy to take down Trump. That it was not Russia after all. Debbie Wasserman Schultz has already threatened the Capital Hill Police chief, on film, that he will suffer "consequences" should he not return the computer equipment. Threats to law enforcement and obstruction of justice are felonies. Take a good look at Debbie Wasseman Schlutz. Does she not look like a reptile?

This is the same old Bush-Clinton criminal conspiracy gang at it again. A criminal conspiracy so far reaching that if finally exposed, it could potentially bring down the entire shadow government. Liberate this nation at last from the Bush-Clinton malignancy. This is a war for ultimate power. Long time Washington observers have noticed, in the wake of all of this, a large number of sewer rats being forced up into the gutters. Caution is urged for visitors to D.C. to be aware of many lower level rats beginning to flee the sinking Bush-Clinton ship of state.

This is a sophisticated, highly coordinated coup attempt. A four way assault between the politicians, the legal system, the media and the intelligence community. It is a criminal conspiracy brought about by real criminals. The whole operation is one gigantic felony, a massive "sting" operation to make it appear that Trump people colluded with the Russians to steal the election. Based on that, Trump already has the constitutional grounds to call for a new government which could spare the nation the tragedy of bloodshed. Washington D.C. is not a swamp. It is a cesspool, a sewer. It is rotten to the core. And God Almighty is going to deal with it. We are fast approaching the most powerful moments in our nation's history. Prophetically, in world history. This power Trump is confronting needs to be understood. The real power behind Bush and Clinton.

I heard it verbalized during the victory of Trump that this signaled the end of Bush and Clinton. As if it was just the passing of the political torch. The end of the Bush-Clinton era. It is much more. This is a struggle for ultimate power. To understand this we need to briefly understand the Bush-Clinton power. While appearing to be political rivals over the years they are in fact, at the root, the same power. Why do you think they have a deep close friendship? Declaring they are "brothers" only with different mothers? In-breeding among the elite class is an old and well known fact. Its a means to maintaining power.

What we have not understood is the nature of that power. The root of that power. Bush and Clinton are descended from the Lucifer-Cain rulers. The elite. They are not human, but humanoid-serpent hybrids. They have a different nature than we normal people have. They have no conscience. No perception of right and wrong. They are extremely low energy, low frequency beings. Do you think Trump knew this when he repeatedly called Jeb Bush "low energy" during the campaign? Being low energy they must prey on others to raise their energy level. Their frequency. They are addicted to conquest. They are hunters. Predators. Chief among their hunting weapons of control, is mind control.

Mind control is the one subject the media will not touch. Really? Higher education is pure indoctrination and the media is pure propaganda, and "mind control" doesn't exist. Give me a break. You see, mind control explains far too many things we see but don't understand. To understand Bush-Clinton I will tell a very revealing story from their sordid past. Before that, to set the stage, lets take a close look at Otto Warmbier, the young student recently returned to the United States from North Korea in a coma, who has since passed away. I can't imagine the family grief and sorrow. Amidst all the talk of an act of war, and U.S. outrage, the truth is probably much deeper. It has all the classic earmarks of a covert mind control operation. The creation of a "Mancherion Candidate", a mind controlled political assassin.

Upon examination by U.S. doctors it was revealed Otto had massive brain damage. It was claimed by the North Koreans that he had been in a coma from the day after he was sentenced to 15 years hard labor for allegedly stealing a propaganda poster. That was some 16 months ago. The timing is very suspicious as it parallels the rise of Trump.

Students of mind control know the CIA imported a Nazi mind control program after World War II and greatly expanded the research in secret underground CIA facilities. It was called "MKUltra" (Mind Kontrol Ultra). Prescott Bush, Poppy's father was a key figure in the program. He helped fund Hitler and the Nazis through his Union Bank and was indicted under the "Trading with the Enemy Act". Like all Bush and Clintons he avoided prosecution. The Bush family is pure CIA, always has been from the beginning of that agency, and mind control is at the heart of black ops, covert operations and assassination. The CIA's first director, Allan Dulles was a Nazi. Prescott Bush was a close confidant. George H.W. Bush headed the operation to overthrow Castro. In this capacity he supervised E. Howard Hunt and the other shooters in Dealey Plaza for the JFK killing. This was all revealed in the "Hoover Memo" from former FBI Director J.Edgar Hoover, which named "Bush of the CIA" Subject: "The JFK Assassination". When the memo surfaced Bush was confronted with it. He denied he was the "Bush" named therein. That he wasn't in the CIA. Really. I guess thats why he was named its director.

There exists today far more circumstantial evidence than necessary for an indictment of Bush in the JFK killing. Most murder cases do not have a "smoking gun" and it is not necessary. If a grand jury today were to hear the evidence against Bush he would be indicted. There is no statute of limitations on murder.

At any rate, during one of the Republican Debates, during the rise of Trump, George H.W. Bush, who was in attendance with Barbara to show support for Jeb, clearly gave the two fingers across the throat, the classic "slit-throat" sign while Trump was on stage. This is universally recognized covert language for assassination. He was signaling "not to worry" to the powers that be that should Trump actually prevail and win, plans were under way to eliminate him. Remember this election was viewed as winner take all, the ultimate and final battle for world power. Prophetically it was. And this will become more clear as we go on.

Meanwhile Otto Warmbier, Bush's assassin-in-training, is suffering in North Korea under mind control programming. Drugs are administered to induce a hypnotic sleep-like suspended animation. Otto is kept in this state for days at a time. Meanwhile low frequency and extra low frequency "triggers" are implanted electronically into the sub conscious via recorded messages he is powerless to stop. "Triggers" that are then activated by his "handler" when it comes time to perform his programmed duty. The human mind is a computer. The program can go on for weeks and months. It is brutal and de-humanizing. The work of sick, demented beasts. If Otto could be programmed to assassinate Trump he could be portrayed by the media as a North Korean sympathizer. A young, bright, idealistic lone nut who had gone over to the other side. Evidence of course is fabricated. Its all too perfect. In the end Otto's brain is severely damaged either through over dose, accident or programming gone bad. Once beyond possible recovery he is returned to the United States to die under claim he had some kind of illness and slipped into a coma from the very beginning. Really.

This is the Bush-Clinton power at work. Cathy O'Brian in her explosive book on mind control "Trance-Formation of America" gives us deep insight into the history of the Bush-Clinton power. Cathy, herself a rescued victim of CIA mind control, recovered her right mind through an auto accident that jarred certain neurological pathways, allowing therapy and prayer in her recovery. She was a mind-controlled "Monarch Slave" serving the very highest political leaders. She tells a story of then Vice President George H.W. Bush and then Governor of Arkansas Bill Clinton. She achieved perfect recall of her then mind controlled state in relating the Bush-Clinton love of something called "The Most Dangerous Game". What she saw, what she heard, exactly what was said.

The story sends chills up the spine. It recounts the two of them, Bush and Clinton, heading off on a hunting expedition . . . of humans. Cathy herself and her then 12 year old daughter were among the hunted. The expedition was at a top secret military base. Two "toy soldiers" (mind controlled special forces) were cut loose along with Cathy and her daughter. Once hunting dogs had Cathy and her daughter easily and quickly pinned down, Bush and Clinton headed off with high powered rifles for what Clinton called "bigger game". After killing one of the soldiers Bush and Clinton brought the other one back and together with Cathy and her daughter headed for a helicopter. Once in the air "The Most Dangerous Game" was completed when, over the lake Bush ordered the remaining soldier to "free fall". Cathy watched in horror as his body hit the water clad in full gear and quickly submerge. Cathy's story has been often corroborated and never challenged.

What did the prophet Daniel see in his dream? A beast government. What are these men if not beasts? Who is the ever present force in American politics since the assassination of JFK? Bush. George Herbert Walker Bush. He would later be joined by Clinton. Clinton forces have always taken orders from Bush forces. But who does Bush work for? The power trying to take down Trump. The seat of world power.

So just what have we established so far? The Bible Code, in revealing events and individuals of our time written into the sub-text of the Old Testament, clearly tells us Sept 11th 2001 was the beginning of "the end of days". The prophet Daniel sees a final world ruling beast government in power at that time. It is Rome. The so-called "fall of the Roman Empire" is a lie. It never fell. It just went underground. The oldest prophecy of all tells us this beast government is run by a "seed of the serpent". A line of elite beasts ruling the world since Cain. We know Bush voted for Hillary. We know Bush-Clinton is at war with Trump. Trump knows the truth of Sept 11th, that it was a Bush-false flag terror event designed to open the back door to war in the Middle East. The criminals want Trump out. One way or another. A coup attempt is underway.

Now lets add a little more. It has been extremely well researched and documented that the war on terror is only the first phase of a terror campaign designed to drive all nations into the arms of a one world government. The second phase will be false flag events designed to appear as astroids and meteors threatening our planet. The campaign for global unity will begin in earnest. On the heels of terror and astroids and meteors, the ultimate off-planet enemy will follow. A false and staged alien attack. A common enemy against which we all must unite. The entertainment industry, news media, and Vatican have been fueling this narrative for decades. Go ahead. Google the Vatican's "Lucifer Project" and the "Blue Beam Project" for reference. Go ahead. The technology is now ready to make it possible. This will drive all nations into the arms of a one world government. Or at least thats their plan.

There is now no doubt, by a convergence of geo-political history and bible prophecy where we are. This brings us to the Joseph Prophecy, the second area of TRUMPROPHECY we must understand.

*   *   *   *   *   *   *

Joseph is a prophecy of the end of days. Hidden in his story is the Joseph Work, what we will call the saving of the nations. And we have to understand that the "end of days" means that corruption in government is coming to an end. "End of days" is good news. It announces that the long held promise of justice flowing like a river, and righteous like a mighty stream, is to be fulfilled very soon!

Joseph, after being driven out, betrayed, defrauded, abandoned, taken into captivity, falsely accused, exiled and imprisoned finds himself uniquely positioned, after the long ordeal, to save the known world through new government policy and sound economic planning. Plans that God gave him directly to deliver to the government. Donald Trump from the beginning has called for getting out of bad regulations and deals that are killing the country, while implementing new policies designed to make America a great nation. A nation with the capacity and wealth to lead other nations, by example, into a new world. He has clearly warned that if we do not change, if we do not implement new policy, our nation will not survive. We will perish in an economic famine. He understands debt. He knows what a tipping point is. But more, he sees the underlying institutional, government, and corporate factors that have led to this moment of truth.

Is Donald Trump leading a "Joseph people" to truly do a "Joseph work"? To save and deliver all nations? To deliver mankind from tyranny and economic collapse? To answer that we need to understand prophetically just who the Joseph people are. Like Joseph, the Joseph people were destined from the beginning to rule the world. To save all nations. Before being granted that privilege and honor however they were to be driven out, betrayed, defrauded, abandoned, taken into captivity, falsely accused, exiled and imprisoned. In other words, humbled.

"Israel" the Joseph People, simply means "ruling with God", or with his authority, his law, on his behalf.   Israel, in the Old Testament, consisted of both the house of Joseph and the house of Judah, collectively called the House of Joseph. It is merely the first nation to be given the Law of God, to enter into covenant with him as a servant people to eventually bring all nations to the glory and honor of that relationship with the Creator. It is about a servant people, not a master race.

The Joseph people would split from the Judah people, and both were taken into captivity. Judah into Babylonian captivity, and Joseph into Assyrian captivity. Judah would eventually return to Zion and re-build the temple. Joseph would never return but be dispersed into the nations of Western Europe and up into Russia. They were white, primarily blond haired and blue eyed. The early migration to found and settle America was overwhelmingly these people. Europe, the United Kingdom, parts of Russia, and The United States are all the same people, the House of Joseph. In time the House of Judah would re-join Joseph and today the United States is the entire and complete House of Joseph, with only remnants remaining in Europe, England, Russia and Palestine. There are more Jews, the House of Judah, along our east coast than in all of Europe and Palestine combined. This is historical fact and facts are stubborn things. (There are other so-called "Israel" nations scattered throughout the world, Canada, New Zealand, Australia, SouthAfrica etc but only America was destined to rule the world representing the entire House of Joseph). While the entire House of Joseph is represented here in America, they have in no way yet, been re-united in the Covenant. Become true brothers once again. Joseph and Judah becoming one in the hand of God is the staggering conclusion of TRUMPROPHECY

The earliest generation of captive Europeans knew exactly who they were. The House of Joseph. And they knew exactly why they had been taken into Assyrian captivity. For breaking the Law of God. In particular, failure to keep Sabbath. But over the succeeding generations they gradually lost sight of their own identity, and embraced utterly pagan rites, rituals, and holidays.   They were led to this apostasy by a religious power that would rise to dominate Europe. It was what Daniel saw as a "little horn" emerging in the midst of the 10 horns (10 nations of Europe) he saw on the final beast government of Rome. A "horn" is always an authority.   It was of course the Roman Catholic Church. The Roman Empire would become the "Holy" Roman Empire. A totally pagan, sun-worshipping religious power of Lucifer himself.   It would teach that the Law of God had been done away with. It was "Sol Invictas" rather, the "sun unconquered" or "in victory". It was pagan sun worship wrapped in Jesus, and they, the Roman Church, spoke exclusively for him and his father, "God" himself. Anyone denying their church authority was denying the authority of "God and his Son". An Inquisition would follow that would drown the nations of Europe in blood leaving upwards of 100 million dead in it's wake. The greatest killing machine in the history of mankind, and not by a little, came wrapped in the New Testament teaching of Jesus. The church killed, using civil executioners, any who did not "believe". Who were declared "heretics". "Anathema" from Christ. All just a cover to kill any daring to resist church authority, the real power of Rome.

The Roman Church through Christianity would also teach that Judah, the Covenant holders remaining true to the Law and Prophets of God, Sabbath Keepers, were the "blind" ones. Not only blind, but the ones who crucified Jesus. This is the spiritual power behind Anti-semitism. And that Christians, mostly the House of Joseph, who "see" Jesus would "save" the world. Get the nations "saved" in the so-called "Great Commission". Then, only after Christians had gone out and saved the known world, would God open the eyes of blind Judah, and bring him in at the last minute. The truth in fact is that when the vast majority of Christians, the House of Joseph, who are "blind" to the Law and Prophets through Christianity, would have their eyes opened to the Covenant, they would then renounce pagan sun worship, Christianity, re-join their Judah brothers, and together save all nations by bringing them gradually into an understanding of God's Covenant. The power of Rome blinded the House of Joseph to the law and prophets and hence to their own identity. It declared the House of Judah to be blind to Jesus and that the Law and Prophets had in fact been done away with. It was now all about Jesus and the Roman Church. It in effect destroyed the power in both houses. It breaks the power of the "holy people" exactly as Daniel foretold.

It is through understanding this power of Rome that breaks the power of the "holy people", that we can then understand Hitler, the Holocaust, the Theology of Master Race and Nazism, the use of racism as strategy, and Anti-semitism. Rome was the real power. Then and now. Remember this is the last beast that the prophet Daniel sees, the last corrupt government to plague planet earth just prior to the Joseph people saving the nations. To understand Rome is to see the ultimate crushing of the serpent seed by the seed of the woman. A fulfillment of the oldest prophecy in the bible. To understand Rome is to see the ultimate struggle for power in the world today as nothing less than Lucifer's last attempt to unify and rule the world. To understand Rome is to see why Donald Trump has stirred up a hornets nest and why there is no going back. It is to grasp why Rome is the seat of world power and how Trump has aroused this power. Why it must take him down or lose it all.

This is the biggest story in the world.

Let me say that again. This is the biggest story in the world and it is just amazing and seemingly impossible that some major documentary filmmaker or journalist has not shocked the world with it. The reason liberal and conservative, Democrat and Republican, deep state, media, intelligence, educational, and entertainment forces have united as one to savage Trump and take him down is that he has aroused Jesuit power controlling all of them. He has literally taken on the Pope, the Roman Empire in its final stage. We need some brief religious and political history to take TRUMPROPHECY to a deeper level and understand all of this.

To do that we need to look deeper into the prophecy of Daniel which informs us that the Roman Empire has not fallen yet.   Rome never fell, it just went into covert operations to rule the world. It fell from the visible and comprehendible to the hidden and clandestine. It unwittingly and unintentionally aroused critical thinkers all over the world. Those who read, study and think critically. Those who see big events and simple slogans and mantras as instruments of manipulation to create mass hysteria, fear, and a desired geo-political outcome. Those who protect their mind and personal judgments, who see them as their God-given right to liberty of conscience. By reading this, or listening to TRUMPROPHECY, you hopefully have joined us.

Rome, from the Pope's throne in the Vatican, controls the world. Simple? If you have a problem with this you need to take it up with the Prophet Daniel. Rome is the final beast empire to rule this world. Yeah, it is so simple that the world's population has run right past it. Been totally deceived. And the world's staged media is the major pawn in this game. It has allowed Rome to mire the nations in militarism, war, fear and terror for far too long. And how about this: It controls the United States as well. How? The Act of 1871 changed the U.S. Constitution from The Constitution FOR the United States to The Constitution OF The United States.

With passage of The Act of 1871 a city state (a state within a state) called the District of Columbia located on 10 sq miles of land in the heart of Washington was formed with its own flag and its own independent constitution - the United States' secret second constitution. (And by the way the Vatican sits on 10 sq miles of land within Rome and operates as its' own separate and sovereign country. A coincidence? No. Its the same secret world-ruling government.) The flag of Washington's District of Columbia has 3 red stars, each symbolizing a city state within the three city empire. The three city empire consists of Washington D.C., City of London Corporation, and Vatican City State. City of London Corporation is the corporate center of the three city states and controls the world economically. Washington D.C. is in charge of the military, and the Vatican controls it all under the guise of spiritual guidance. Although geographically separate, the city states of: City of London Corporation, the Vatican, and the District of Columbia are one interlocking empire called "Empire of the City". This arrangement allows the District of Columbia to operate as a Vatican corporation outside the original constitution of the United States in total disregard of the best interests of the American people. This is the power Donald Trump is REALLY confronting. POTUS, the acronym for President Of The United States, means "vassal king". A vassal is a subordinate, or servant of a superior power. The president serves Rome. The U.S. government is run by Jesuit priests from the bowels of Georgetown University. There is actually a picture of Bill Clinton on his knees to the Jesuit High Command at Georgetown. Bill Clinton knows what happened to JFK. JFK, A Roman Catholic, announced during his candidacy; "I am not the Catholic candidate for president, I am the Democratic Party candidate for president. I do not speak for the church, and the church does not speak for me". He sent an "America first" message. The order to take him down originated in the Vatican.

Whether Trump is aware of this is unknown but he no doubt understands he is up against an entrenched power structure. In reality there is no difference between political power and religious power. There is only a central and unified real power that operates in certain and absolute immunity behind both masks. God, in his time and way will unmask it. How it came to be is one of the great and fascinating stories of all history. Its one we need to briefly understand as adapted from an article entitled "Forged Origins of The New Testament".

The merging of political and religious power in the world came about because the Roman Emperor Constantine, a pagan sun-worshipper, wanted absolute control over the Roman Empire. He was a pragmatic and ruthless ruler who was tired of religious factions in strife and warfare throughout the empire. To consolidate his rule he convened a council, the Council of Nicaea in 325AD to come up with a single pagan deity for the entire empire, thereby eliminating the on-going religious wars. The meeting was actually convened on the summer solstice June 21st. It was to honor the sun god. He had been initiated into the pagan religious order of Sol Invictus, ("sun in victory", a label still carried by the Roman Church to this day) in 321AD. Church history tells us he converted to "christianity" in 312AD to fit a different narrative. There is no contemporary historical evidence that indicates this.   It would be impossible to convert to a religion that did not exist at the time. Even if it had, and even if it were true, he must have gotten "unsaved", un-converted, in 321AD to convert to sun worship. So you see, when the dates don't work, and the math does not add up, you have a problem with the narrative. You have an honesty problem. Its called a lie. Then the lie gets picked up by teachers over time and established as "truth". Thats how it works.

So when the dust settled after some 18 months, all the delegates to the council still could not agree on a single god for the whole empire so Constantine decided the issue for them. From the British west he chose the great Druid god, Hesus, and from the east he chose Krishna, sanskrit for christ. Hence Hesus-Krishna became the new Roman god. Centuries later when "J" was added to the alphabet the name subsequently evolved into Jesus Christ, Jesus is a Roman word that means "I am".

Both pagan divinities had become one god by Roman apotheosis decree which was ratified by a vote of 161 to 157. This act of political deification "effectively and legally placed Hesus Krishna among the Roman gods as one individual composite". All the amalgamated pagan doctrines from east and west found a single earthly incarnation in Hesus Krishna. After the new Roman god was decided upon, all the religious texts of the meeting were culled for appropriate testimonies. Whatever was "good" was included. Whatever was "evil" was discarded. Call me crazy but it sounds like they were partaking of the "tree of the knowledge of good and evil". Constantine commanded a work that "would astonish". The ultimate god of the ultimate religion, representing the ultimate empire must be spectacular, an astonishing god. Nothing less would suffice. In doing so a religious power was created that had the ultimate authority, God himself, in the person of Jesus, and hence the emperor. It became the ultimate political sword. To question Rome or the Emperor would be to question "God" himself and no one would dare to do that. This is the origin of the "divine right of kings". It established the ultimate dictatorship, a two headed monster of both religious and political dominion. Look at the politicians today holding a bible in one hand and waving a flag with the other.

So Constantine commanded this religious book which veiled his political authority. A single bound volume was assembled by the scribes and submitted for the emperor's approval. It created a religious dictatorship. These were the "new testimonies" which became the new testament.   It was called the "book of books" as the single volume contained bits and pieces of many volumes. It put all authority in the hands of the "state-church" and established the bishops as the only spokesman for the new god. The Roman name for "book of books' is biblica, or bible. Constantine then made it the official "Word of the Roman God" throughout the empire in the hopes of avoiding any further religious wars. That was eventually shortened to the Word of God, with the combined testimonies as the New Testament. All other writings were destroyed. Anyone caught with any other writings or teachings was beheaded on order of the emperor. The spirit of the eventual blood thirsty Inquisition, the greatest killing machine ever loosed upon the nations, later to arise in full bloom under the Papacy, was also birthed at the council with this Imperial decree of death to anyone holding any other belief or teaching. Church authority had the civil arm of execution, the state, behind it from the beginning.

But we have been told a different story haven't we? We have been told that Constantine, with his conversion embraced Christianity and made it the religion of the empire. And that while he may have added a few pagan trappings, he saw a vision of the cross and was led to "conquer in this sign". That he granted official toleration to persecuted Christians. That he was the great champion of christianity. That he was even a type of Christ. This is all contrary to historical fact and even the Catholic authorities say it should be stricken and erased from their literature forever. Why? Because they wouldn't want their church to be viewed as the real power behind the sword of civil authority. Simply put, there was no Christian religion at the time for Constantine or anyone else to embrace. It came with the meeting, the council of Nicaea as a composite pagan religion with the object to quell warring religious factions throughout the empire, to solidify civil authority! It was not even called "Christianity" until the 15th century!

The oldest bible was discovered by Dr. Constantin (how ironic) Von Tischendorf (1815-1847). The Sinai Bible became the obsession of Tischendorf. He was a pious German biblical scholar who devoted his life to studying the origins of the New Testament. By the time he was done he had generated some 15,000 pages of notes on the Sinai Bible. This pious and dedicated man, eventually greatly disillusioned at his study concluded: "It seems the personage of Jesus Christ was made narrator for many religions". In other words he was an allegorical construct to represent a composite pagan theology, not an historical figure. He further stated, "We must frankly admit that we have no source of information with respect to the life of Jesus Christ other than the ecclesiastic writings assembled during the fourth century". A staggering conclusion based upon massive research!

Professor Edmond S. Bordeaux, after spending several years in the Vatican Archives concluded that the whole of church history is nothing more than a retroactive fabrication. He said, "The church anti-dated all her late works, some newly made, some revised and some counterfeited, which contained the final expression of her history . . . her technique was to make it appear that much later works written by Church writers were composed a long time earlier, so that they might become evidence of the first, second, or third centuries". Religious treachery. Plain and simple.

Frederic Farrar of Trinity College, Cambridge, who wrote The Life Of Christ says, "It is amazing that history has not embalmed for us even one certain or definite saying or circumstance in the life of the Saviour of mankind . . . there is no statement in all history that says anyone saw Jesus or talked with him. Nothing in history is more astonishing than the silence of contemporary writers about events relayed in the four Gospels".

If Jesus Christ had been born of a virgin the news would have been so fantastic and confirmed by so many that he would have been watched and written about since the day of his birth. He would have been a cultural icon no matter what people believed. The Roman Empire itself would have tracked him, as a potential threat to the state but not a single government record exists. Yet at age 30 in Mark's Gospel he just suddenly appears out of nowhere, and even the locals allegedly asked if he was the one, or should they look for another? Wouldn't they have known him, and known him well after being around for some 30 years ?!!

The point is, the Roman Church, and by extension the Protestant Church, is asking mankind today to accept a politically deified saviour and the shadowy writings concocted at a pagan conclave, under orders of a sun worshipping Emperor, some three centuries beyond the time in question, as evidence of truth regarding the biggest issue man faces, eternal truth. The point is the Roman Church, by its own admission and the evidence of multitudes of researchers, scholars and archivists, interpolated even the original shadowy writings, even attaching names to the gospels that do not represent real people. The point is we have absolutely no contemporary government, cultural, artistic, literary, biographical, musical or personal historical evidence from the first century for a Christ that today some 2 billion people are believing for their eternal salvation.

The point is the Roman Church that has sold this Jesus to mankind sits today as the foremost political, religious and financial power in the world, with a sordid, dark and blood drenched story unmatched by any institution in world history.

Constantine died in 337AD.   He had left his mark on the world. Hesus Krishna, Jesus the Christ, a politically expedient amalgamated theological merging of pagan gods, along with an astonishing body of esoteric and mystical pagan writings, presented as the new testimonies, had morphed into a new religious system! All the pagan mystery religions of the old Roman Empire told the "Jesus story" under different pagan names. A thousand years before they merged into the Jesus story. The monster of apostasy, the final phase of the Roman Empire foretold by Daniel the prophet, which he saw as a "little horn" on the final beast, a two headed religious and political empire, an unnatural beast, had surfaced in history. By 349AD the Pope took for himself the name "papa" Latin for father. The "Papa-cy" had come.

No other figure on planet earth rivals the Pope in stature. There certainly is no Jewish rabbi, or Muslim cleric or Christian pastor his equal. Even Billy Graham kissed his ring. He dwarfs all world leaders. He is swooned over and lauded by the world's press. He speaks for "God" himself, and only he alone can save us all. Yet his authority all stands or falls on Jesus the Christ who was invented as a legal, political, religious and financial construct in the early part of the fourth century. Pope Leo X (1513-1521AD) called christ a "fable". He said, "How well we know what a profitable superstition this fable of Christ has been for us". "For us" for the power of Rome. This is from the Pope himself, the so-called head of the Christian church worldwide! Some 2 billion people who call themselves believers, and who have staked their salvation on this belief.

This power has been historically unfathomable and unstoppable. It spreads out into the nations via a network of Jesuit priests. Like a metastasizing cancer. A global malignancy. Read "The Secret History of the Jesuits" and "Vatican Assassins" for reference. This is the real power Donald Trump is confronting. Seated in the one place mankind would never suspect, the Vatican. Hiding behind religious theatre and pomp and circumstance. Now Hillary Clinton's reliance on a Jesuit Priest for spiritual guidance begins to take on more ominous meaning. Now Tim Kaine's (Cain's?) praise for the Jesuits begins to make more sense. You know, those who educated and inspired him. Lucifer's legions again and always at work.   It is the same old Cain humanoid-serpent hybrids posing as leaders whose only mission in life is the good of the people. Really.

With this historical background on Lucifer's seat of power in the world, lets now bring it up into the modern era to understand Hitler, his Nazism and Master Race Theology, the Holocaust, racism as a strategy, and Anti-semitism. All really pretty simple once you see it.

The clash between Trump and those of "the resistance" is nothing less than the Law of God verses Lucifer. This is the essence of TRUMPROPHECY. A battle between the seed of the woman and the seed of the serpent, with the seed of the woman finally becoming wise to the serpent and rising to crush it, demanding justice worldwide. Between a God and law centered theology, and a Luciferian strategy to move the world into the tyranny of a one world dictatorship. This is expressed in many different ways geo-politically as basic Americanism vs Progressivism.

Hitler was a pawn and tool of the Vatican. Look at a World War II map of Europe occupied by the Third Reich. Notice how Italy, until the end, was not. Why? Because Mussolini also had a concordat, a "formal agreement" a "covenant" with the Vatican. Do you know what a concordat is? It is an agreement between the Pope and a government on "church matters". It specifies what a government will do to obey the Pope. The Act of 1871 is a "concordat". It specifies what the United States will do to obey Rome. So Mussolini had a concordat with the Vatican. He was also a pawn and tool of the Pope. Even after Mussolini was brushed aside and Italy became Nazi occupied, the Vatican was never touched. Remember the scene from the movie "Patton" when the American Army liberated Italy? What did Patton do? He walked up a long flight of stairs and kissed the Pope's ring.

The war was also a great opportunity for the Vatican to increase their financial position. The Vatican, under cover of medical transports, literally raped Europe of gold, sliver, precious gems and art treasure worth untold billions. Today, worth much more. The Allied and Axis soldiers did not touch these transports. They were allowed to pass under humanitarian/medical guise through the midst of it all. It set up the Vatican after the war as the greatest financial power on earth. It was the greatest heist in the history of the world. They even extracted the gold fillings from the teeth of Jews before they sent them to the ovens. It was the Vatican, hiding behind Hitler, that really did it. Read "Vatican Billions" for reference. The many nuns and priests who worked to ease the suffering during the war had no idea what their master in Rome was all about. They were, and are to this day, tragic pawns of a merciless power struggle for world control.

Hitler's famous SS troops were modeled after the Jesuits. Their oath to the Fuhrer was very similar to the Jesuit oath to the church, "to kill and shed the blood of all unbelievers". Pope Francis is a Jesuit. He has taken the blood oath. And by the way the Jesuit-blood oath they take includes child sacrifice. In the catacombs beneath the alters of Cathedrals all over this world are the slain bodies of children. No pastor or Christian leader in America has ever touched this story. Why? Because they are all part of it. Go ahead, Google the Jesuit Oath, but be warned it is horrific. Go ahead. The Holocaust, and in fact World War II, was just the Vatican Inquisition carried forward, except this time the target was not just believers in Jesus and nation states in Europe who would not submit to Rome's authority, it was a Roman church who would not submit to God's authority, and saw the Jews as representing God's law and prophets. Lucifer knew full well who the true covenant holders were. The Vatican did not give a damn whether anyone believed in their "Jesus". It was about church authority. "Jesus" was just a weapon of mind control.

If Jesus was truly the son of God, and the Pope is literally "God" on earth, then how could the Papacy kill tens of millions of believers in Jesus? How could it slaughter the Jews? God's Chosen People.   Have we lost our God given ability to think?

Why did Hitler go after the Jews? The Vatican knew the true covenant holders, destined by God to rule the world, must be eliminated for Lucifer's minions, people like Bush and Clinton, a counterfeit "master race" of white elites, to rule the world.   Lucifer, through the Vatican made war against the "holy people" of God. Exactly as Daniel fore-told!   It was a master Lucifer scheme to eliminate God's true covenant holders, the Jews, and replace them with his own carefully crafted counterfeits! Hitler's Aryan Master Race. Lucifer carefully wrapped the Holocaust in the larger package of World War II. It allowed the commission of such despicable acts of crimes against humanity, in the name of a Master White Race Theology, that anything smacking of "white privilege" or, anyone daring to tell the true "Joseph Story" would subsequently be howled and screamed at by the thought police as "politically incorrect". A racist. A hater of people. A criminal. It was Lucifer's grand scheme to neutralize and destroy the true Judah peo-ple for good, eliminating any possibility of re-unification with the House of Joseph. Luci-fer's "final solution", the extermination of the House of Judah, was to prevent the coming of the Kingdom of God! Lucifer was paving the way for his own world rule. A very close counterfeit, at least initially. Lucifer knows only God's law has the power to save the na-tions and bring about the Kingdom of God. He also knows that when Joseph and Judah re-unite he is finished.

So today we have a white, blonde haired, blue eyed President Trump. An actual son of the House of Joseph. On the other hand we have a Lucifer inspired explosion of race baiting. The most sensitive and explosive word in the world today is . . . race. Any truth spoken by anyone, anywhere, about anything is immediately destroyed by hurling the "R" word.   Pretty simple strategy to keep the truth from being heard. And if you are white, or even hold an anglo saxon historical perspective on the Western Democracies, then you need to hang your head in shame and apologize for your "white privilege". And why shouldn't the world hate you for being white after what Hitler did? After what the Klu Klux Klan did to black people? No pun intended, but the KKK has been, from the beginning, a Jesuit black op (on the political level the terrorist arm of the Democratic Party) with the goal of creating race wars. Imagine the world wide shock when it is learned the Jesuits were behind it all along. You know, the "holy" church in Rome. Yeah, thats the one.   So now its easy to portray President Trump and those who love and support him as . . . Nazis. Racists. White Supremacists. KKK lovers. Fascists. Makes perfect sense.

The real enemy of mankind has not yet been revealed. When he is, it will be the theological, political, and racial epicenter of a world wide earthquake. So let me clarify something here. Both Mussolini and Hitler declared their hatred for Christianity. So you might ask how they could be working for the church? We know that behind the scenes they worked hand in glove with the Vatican through the Jesuit High Command. They were legally bound to the Vatican through political concordats. They were the principal agents of Inquisition II. Remember how we established that the Vatican always used civil executioners during the Inquisition and how they want their connection to Constantine to be expunged from their history? Why? They don't want to be seen as the real power behind the sword. If Hitler and Mussolini were not "haters of Christianity" then they would not have had the cover needed to deceive the world. To never suspect the connection. Setting up a controlled opposition through which you can draw out your enemies and accomplish your goals really originated with the Jesuits. Its part of their manifesto. A guiding principal. Lucifer has been around a long time.

Today Lucifer has everyone just where he wants them. Its called Identity politics and National Socialism. Can you imagine that? Where have we heard National Socialism before? Oh yeah, National Socialism means. . . are you ready? . .are you really ready? . . .National Socialism means Nazism!!   National Socialism is Nazism! So thats where we've heard that before. Oh yeah, it was that guy Hitler. Wait a minute. Hitler was bad. . . but National Socialism, Nazism. . . is good? Whats going on here? Could it be that Sanders and Clinton and Bush and those manipulating the left and the right, are in truth the REAL Nazis? The REAL fascist-racists hiding behind Identity politics?? Hey, what do you know, the Bush family and the Walker (Barbara) family were deeply involved in the eugenics movement, you know, the one to create a master race of white people. Wow, what a coincidence. I guess there was more to the Bush involvement with Hitler than we realized.

Why would the Bush family be such big supporters of Hitler and so prominent in the importing of the Nazi High Command to the United States to form the CIA and NASA after the war? Well, it just so happens that the Bush-CIA runs the drug-running-Iran-Contra-covert shadow government, a free standing global criminal conspiracy, of which the Clinton Foundation is an arm, and NASA will bring mankind the final staged and fake alien invasion. Go ahead. Google the Vatican "Lucifer Project" and NASA's "Blue Beam Project". They are the same thing. Both exist to bring in the final dictatorship. Drive the nations into the waiting arms of a one world government. What George H. W. Bush would announce to the world in his 1991 State Of The Union Address as a "New World Order". A Third Reich. Imagine that, a Nazi strategy all along. I guess the-Nazis in Europe lost the war, but the real Nazis here in America, and hidden in Rome, have been winning ever since. Sure looks that way to me.

So lets be real clear here before we move on. National Socialism is Nazism. It is not Venezuela or even Cuba. It is Nazi Germany. America is positioned today where Germany was in 1939, just before Hitler unleashed hell. National Socialism is the governing model for a Fascist. It is cradle to grave dependance on the state. It is a theology. The state becomes "God". Didn't Hitler say he was married to Germany and that is why he could not marry Eva Braun? By extension then the people become married to "God", the state. It is their husband, the provider of their every need. The very source of life itself that will end all injustice in the population. The reality is that once power is achieved the nation quickly degenerates into a super elite class, and a slave population. Sound familiar? Those fit to serve the elites are kept around, to replenish the workers and do the work. The rest are eliminated.

Now here is a chilling warning which is another motivation for writing TRUM-PROPHECY. You need to consider this very carefully. Bernie Sanders was trotted out as a Bush-Clinton puppet to dump National Socialism on the country as a political ideal to end all injustice once and for all. To solve all our problems. He was a pawn to move the narrative to the far left, something Hillary could not do in an outright fashion right out of the gate. It provided her the cover to move to her true Fascist roots, her deeply held radical theology, from which she could then pick up the torch, once they had brushed the phony Bernie Sanders aside. Now she becomes the underdog champion of the people. They thought it would sweep her into office. IT STILL CAN, OR, THE NEXT BUSH-CLINTON PUPPET IN LINE. Even the possible return of Bernie Sanders. The cry for Socialism aroused the single largest voting block in this country, the millennial generation. Not one of these young people, not one, anywhere in this country, can even define Socialism. They think it will end economic and political injustice for everyone be-cause that is what they have been told. Yet not one of them, not one, has a clue. Re-member these are the college educated among us. This is exactly how Adolph Hitler rose to power except he did it with the entire population. Dictatorship via democracy with the hidden puppet master tucked away in Rome. Its not new. All they need is a majority. Now they have it. The Bernie Sanders "revolution" the socialist cry for political and economic justice, is a masterpiece of manipulation. I will not sit by and witness America sink into dictatorship without doing all I can. TRUMPROPHECY is all I can do. I pray this warning is sounded all over this nation. My fellow Americans, you have been warned.

So lets move on. Could it be that the politics of Identity and Progressivism, al-legedly all about tolerance and diversity, is really just a cover for some power mad rac-ists, some Fascists made in the image of Hitler, who are bent on submerging America under a sea of National Socialism? Could it be? Yeah, that might explain the hatred for all things Trump. You see, the progressives don't really care if you are man or woman, white or black, rich or poor, or really anything else. And if you are LGBT, don't kid your-self. You will be among the first to be eliminated when they achieve power, along with their perverted pedophile priesthood stretching around the globe. You are just a pawn to an agenda. Another medium of manipulation. You won't produce workers for them. Only THEY can be LGBT. Its not about what you believe. Or who you are. Or how you identify yourself. Its about what they believe. Its about who they are. Its about power for themselves. A white master race. Nothing new here.

Where Hitler failed, Hillary will succeed. From Hitler to Hitllar-y looks like to me. No wonder Hitllar-y loves the Jesuits! They hold her ticket to rule. And its the same old ticket. Promise the people everything. Get elected. Consolidate power, one dead body at a time. One pay-for-play scheme at a time. Control the propaganda, the media. Render the congress impotent. Slowly build a global network of corruption. Hide be-hind a charitable foundation. Keep shouting democracy while the dictatorship is laid one brick at a time. As a Fascist, spawn an anti-fascist movement to attack those who are not. Exploit race. Incite class warfare. Use real and imagined injustice to divide and conquer. And when its finally too late for the people, step from behind the curtain. Or should I say from behind the long flowing robes of his majesty at the Vatican.

And let me say something here. As killing machines go, the Catholic Inquisition and Communism killed far more people than Fascism. So why is Fascism the ideology of choice to achieve the ultimate dictatorship? There are two tracks here. First, the real Fascists pose as champions of the people and use the fascist label to attack those who are not. They claim to be "anti-fascists". This puts all opposition on its heels having to defend their every word and deed. Everyone else is guilty right out of the gate. Second, Fascism is tied to an abhorrent, horrific Master White Race Theology. You can't use the Inquisition or Communism to exploit and manipulate race on your path to power. To divide and conquer. But a Hitler-Master-White-Race Theology comes in pretty handy when its all about identity and diversity and tolerance. When its all about exploiting identity and race.

George W. Bush lives in a posh North Dallas neighborhood that forbids minority ownership. By restrictive covenant. Look where George H. W. Bush lives. Look where the Clintons live. How many minorities, struggling or otherwise, vacation in the Hamptons at $10,000/week? None. And Lucifer has deceived these humanoid-serpents that they are destined to rule the world in immortality once they succeed in gaining total power. The process of gaining dictatorship of the entire world is their proving ground. Where they show the master, Lucifer, and his puppet sitting on the throne in the Vatican, they are truly worthy. In the end, what these people don't understand, is that they too will be eliminated. Thats the destiny of those who sell their souls for power. Because for Lucifer of old, they must keep coming, or be devoured by him.

So you see, its all really simple isn't it? If you are a Fascist, a Lucifer disciple posing as a champion of the people then you need a strategy of deception to move yourself into a position to rule the world. (Wasn't Ben Carson concerned about Hillary being a Lucifer disciple? Isn't she a disciple of Saul Alinsky who dedicated his radical manifesto, Rules For Radicals, to Lucifer himself? Do the math. Wasn't it openly discussed during the election?) So thats what this is all about. Who rules. God's Joseph people, or Lucifer's master race counterfeits? Thats why there are two ideologies, in fact two theologies now before mankind. Moses has come down off the mountain and split the nation wide open. Let those who are on the Lord's side come and embrace the Law and Prophets of God. Let those who are on Lucifer's embrace the lawlessness of Identity politics and Progressivism. Nothing but a vicious racism. Dictatorship wrapped in diversity. Let them stay lost in false religions that have mired the world in war and human trafficking since ancient Babylon. There is no middle ground.

Now we can see why God is bringing forth a Joseph people to do a Joseph work. Why all hell has broken loose. Why God has brought us President Trump. Because its time. Because it is the end of days. The days of corruption and beast government.

The final pathetic last gasp of Bush-Clinton fascist politicians doing black ops for the Vatican. But they are not going down without a fight to the death. What they don't know, is that it will be theirs. Its over.

The Joseph people, blinded to their own identity by losing sight of the law and prophets of God, can now see again. They can shake off the false religion of the Roman church, and forget their captivity.   They can embrace their Judah brothers and together become one in the hand of God. Finally and at long last ready to serve mankind and heal the nations by raising up the law and prophets to the people of all races. Leading all people to the promised land. The cry for justice is being heard in all nations. God has answered in America first, with raising Donald Trump. He is calling out injustice and corruption all over the world. It has begun. This is a theological and political earthquake and it is sending shock waves down the corridors of power in the church and government. It will no longer be restrained. God is going to rescue all people, all of mankind, from the false religious and political shepherds. They will face condemnation.

And before I get attacked for advancing a servant race of white, anglo-saxon leaders, let me state that the Covenant of God is not some exclusive club. Anyone. . . anyone who joins themselves to God by Covenant will be honored by the Creator, and be part of this great work. This Joseph work. It is not race exclusive but the enemies of God want mankind to think so.   Anyone can be an honored servant of the truth. It even states that anyone not of the House of Joseph who joins themselves by Covenant to God, will be given a name even higher than that of sons and daughters! So, you see, global racism dies when the truth at last becomes known. Wars between religions, you know, killing unbelievers, and race hatred cloaked in identity politics, then spewed as progressivism, are at last exposed for what they are, vicious racist strategies to divide and conquer the world. God is just a little bit smarter than Lucifer and all his minions. And the people, you know, Muslim, Christian, Jew, Hindu, Old Testament, agnostic, and atheist, those who do not yet see our Creator, all of us, mankind, we are ready for some relief. Ready for that glorious day when nation shall not lift up sword against nation, and neither shall they learn war anymore. Ready to acknowledge to one another that we are all God's children. And we are ready to hug one another. And dance, and laugh again.

Please forgive a personal note on this. I am a 64 year old white man. The greatest compassion and humanity I have ever experienced came from an old black man I met one day. With honest eyes and trembling hands he asked me what religion I was, what church I went to. I told him I didn't, that I just tried to study the bible to know what the truth was. He asked me why everything "good" was white and everything "bad" was black. He was on his own search for truth. . . I told him I didn't have any answers. I just told him one day the love of God will overcome the religions of man. He leaned close to me and just above a whisper said, "Spend the day with me". He was probably lonesome and just wanted some company.

As we talked, we laughed together, and I cried. When lunch was served his plate came first. A simple tuna sandwich and some grapes. He told me to take some. I took a small one. He leaned over and whispered, "Get some big ones". We ate in silence for a time and he was aware I had traveled a great distance. He leaned over and whispered, "I'll put you up in a motel tonight". It was like, "I love ya brother, I got ya covered". Life had been a long journey for both of us through the pain and trouble of this nation. I was an upper middle class college educated white man, he was a kind and generous black man from the streets who had experienced severe racial and religious persecution. Yet here we were breaking bread. And he was offering to help me. This was not religion. This was the love of God overcoming religion.

He was a Muslim, and told me he suffered from Parkinsons. After lunch we visited for couple more hours. As the afternoon wore on a gentle rain began to fall. When he attempted to get up from his chair he had to rock forward enough to stand up. Parkinsons had taken a great toll on him. I reached out to him with a reverse grip and pulled him up and to my chest. We stood frozen in time for a couple seconds.

We then headed for a love seat where he patted for me to sit next to him. In a few minutes he began to get drowsy and finally drifted off to sleep. I guess the time had come for his afternoon nap. As I got up to leave he woke up and reached out with a trembling hand to say goodbye. Leaving his kindness and gentleness and love was hard for me. I've always kind of felt like a nobody in this world. But with him I felt like somebody. I realized as I drove away what a gift he had, to make people who feel like nobody, feel like somebody. His name, was Muhammad Ali.

I miss you champ. And can't wait to see you again someday soon. The world so desperately needs your gift. We need to dance, and laugh again.

Thank you for letting me share this story. Somehow it just seemed to fit in all of this. Ali had given me another gift as well. A list of "Bible Contradictions" that had been compiled by some Islamic scholars. Studying those contradictions became a search for truth. A search into the truth, or lie, of the New Testament. A search that led me to the truth of the JFK killing. A search that led all the way to the mother of all lies at the Vatican. It set me free from religion, the church, and a fable called Jesus. I am forever grateful to Muhammad Ali. I am forever liberated from the mother whore in Rome, and all her daughter harlot Protestant churches. My prayer is that hundreds of millions, all over the world, will soon be set free as well.

We can now return to our narrative and see why the Roman/Protestant Church advances a false teaching of prophecy called "Futurism". You know, the one where the Roman Empire reforms in Europe and an anti-christ arises at it's head to rule the world? Sometime in a future 7 year tribulation period, at the beginning of which the "church" gets to escape it all in a prior "rapture". You know the one. It keeps people blinded to the dictator sitting in the Vatican who continues to tighten the noose of dictatorship around the neck of all nations. It keeps people divided and asleep, numb to the increasing evidence that something is radically wrong in the world, and it is our responsibility to address it. It spawns the delusion that when it all goes bad we can just hit the rapture button and get an instant eject from all the trouble. Why should we care anyway?

On the other hand, the Joseph Prophecy, if we apply it to the rise of Trump, means we may experience 7 years of plenty, followed by 7 years of famine. What does this mean if we apply it to our time? We already see evidence that we may in fact be in for 7 good years under Trump. The stock market is soaring. Corporate money is being repatriated back in to the United States. Regulations are being rolled back. Jobs and companies are coming back home. We are getting out of international and regional trade deals bad for the United States.   But most of all we have a president who understands business, and has increasingly put people in charge to make America wealthy. Didn't Joseph do the exact same thing? He undoubtedly had many at every level of government to implement his economic agenda. Don't you think the surrounding nations looked upon the stored wealth of food in Egypt, the result of Joseph's economic plan, as true wealth when the famine came? It became the power to sustain life itself.

What does this story foretell? The power to get wealth is granted by God for one purpose and one purpose only. To establish his Covenant. Donald Trump has talked repeatedly of making America wealthy. If we consider a 7 year "famine" period to follow the next 7 years of "plenty" we can see our "Joseph nation" positioned, in the 8th year of a Trump presidency in the "wealth of the covenant" sufficient for other nations to come to America for the purpose of developing their own programs for prosperity. Natural resource development, infrastructure, jobs, training, cooperation instead of competition. A new paradigm. Shared wealth based on productivity not redistribution. And the national capacity to help other nations harvest their own wealth. Everyone with hope of a better future. In other words we become a model for other nations of the world to follow. But it would not just be the national programs they would be coming for, but the foundation in God's laws on which the programs would be built. This is an exact fulfillment of many prophecies and the description of how God's Kingdom will slowly spread to the entire world! It is hard to imagine, if Trump succeeds, that we are not witnessing the dawn of true national hope. For the first time. For real.

Trump is despised and hated by liberals and conservatives because he is not full of ideology. In fact he has none. Not like the political group thinker who is controlled by hidden forces, who goes on TV and tells us again and again how their particular brand of ideology will save us. He calls people out, tells it like it is. Hits back at hypocrisy. Refuses to have his words and intentions garbled in transmission. He is a problem solver. A Joseph. He understands that a problem has an underlying cause, usually corruption, that must be dealt with. That means he is going to be a problem for a lot of people. And that means he is some sort of divine instrument of correction leading the early stages of a national reformation. It is nothing less. I am 64 years old and never thought I would see it in my lifetime.

The purpose of TRUMPROPHECY is to see the truth that the law and prophets of God allow us to see. That we might awaken to the massive deception gripping the nations. But most of all to give us hope, to see Donald Trump as an instrument of that hope sent to our nation at this moment of history.   And this brings us to the third area of ancient prophecy bearing on TRUMPROPHECY. Timing. There is a prophecy that we have not understood because it was sealed until our time. It is again, in Daniel. It deals with the specific moment the end of the "wonders" that Daniel had been shown would come. In other words the end of the beast governments. It is signaled as a time when people, mankind, the seed of the woman, would witness the end of corruption on earth and the dawn of righteousness in government. Become happy. Can we even imagine such a thing? No more terror. No more war. Dancing in the streets. Perfect strangers embracing and hugging each other as they did in the streets of America and Europe at the end of World War II. Except this time it is not the end of a World War. This time, it is the end of war in the world. So lets consider this prophecy of timing.

*　　*　　*　　*　　*　　*　　*

Daniel asks the angel Gabriel to understand the great mystery of the empires he saw rise and fall over time, and when the end of the beast governments would be. The end of "these wonders".   He was given a specific answer. He was told it would be 1,290 days (years in prophetic terms) from when the perpetual sacrifice was taken away, and the abomination of desolation set up. Two things. The sacrifice taken away, and an abomination of desolation set up.

The perpetual sacrifice was the day the High Priest would go into the Holy of Holies to make an annual atonement, with the blood of a slain goat, for the sins of the nation. The blood of the slain goat was offered up to God as a sin offering, and then the sins of the people were symbolically laid upon the head of a live goat who was then driven into the wilderness. It was a two part annual atonement for the nation. The Bush CIA is now making the Muslim people a scape goat for Sept 11th. All the Muslim people world wide are now being blamed and exploited by the Bush-Clinton power to hide the truth of Sept 11th.

We have previously established that Sept 11th was the beginning of the "end of days" so we have the current geo-political picture of Daniel's ancient prophecy. We have the general timing. The Bible Code, written 3,000 years ago tells us Sept 11th was the beginning of the "end of days". But can we be more specific? Yes!

An abomination of desolation is something that would deny a nation access to God. Thats it. So we have to look in history for something that would rise to that level, to fulfill Daniel's prophecy. We should not be surprised that both Christianity and Islam took away the sacrifice and set up the abomination. The Papacy emerged in history in the 4th century. About 250 years later, in 685AD the Muslims overran the Holy Land. At that time they began construction of The Dome of the Rock, on the temple mount, as a shrine to their victory. The Dome of the Rock, which would eventually become a mosque, a holy place of worship to Muslims, was under construction for several years and finally completed in 691AD.

Along with the Vatican in Rome, upon completion, the Dome of the Rock would end worship of the true and living God on earth. It deceives the Muslims, but it also bars the Joseph and Judah people from the annual Day of Atonement.   It "broke the power of the holy people" exactly as foretold in Daniel's prophecy. The Dome of the Rock is built on the exact spot, the Holy of Holies, where the Day of Atonement was performed. So the Christian Papacy removed the law and prophets from the House of Joseph, and the Muslim Dome of the Rock removed the perpetual sacrifice from the House of Judah by setting up an "abomination", something that would bar access to the site of the national annual atonement.

Daniel is told there will be 1,290 years from the time the perpetual sacrifice is taken away and the abomination of desolation is set up, (the Day of Atonement ceased and the building of the Dome of the Rock was completed) UNTIL the "end of these wonders" the end of the beast governments he had been shown in his dream. He is shown when they would end in history. By 691AD both the Papacy (Christianity) and the Dome of the Rock (Islam) had been set up ending true worship on earth. The Christian Papacy took the Joseph people away from the law and prophets and into pagan sun worship, and the Muslim Dome of the Rock barred access to the Holy of Holies, stopped the Day of Atonement, the perpetual sacrifice for Judah. The power of the holy people, Joseph and Judah, those initially given the Law of God, was broken over the next 1,290 years exactly as Daniel foretold.

Perhaps the reason we have not understood the timing of this is that we have either thought the 1,290 years was an interim period between the cessation of the perpetual sacrifice and the setting up of the abomination, it could be read that way, or we have incorrectly timed the 1,290 years from when the temple was destroyed by the Romans in 70AD, ending the perpetual sacrifice. The dates don't work. In either case we look in history for fulfillment of the prophecy in vain.

The Day of Atonement, the perpetual sacrifice at the temple, officially ended because there was no temple, but the site still remained, even though the sacrifice had ceased with the Roman invasion.   Daniel's prophecy included the setting up of the abomination of desolation over the site, the building of the Dome of the Rock. It did not occur, was not completed until the year 691AD.   From that point forward the prophecy was completed as both had occurred, the sacrifice had ceased, and the shrine barred the site from access. The Joseph-Judah people were henceforth forbidden from praying at the Dome of the Rock. There were other restrictions as well, but that is the one that is central to the prophecy. When construction of the Dome of the Rock was complete, in 691AD, the 1,290 year period of the prophecy could begin counting forward.

So, if we add 1,290 years to 691AD we come to the year 1981AD. What happened in 1981? 1981 began the final chapter of corruption in our government. A transition period. It was the beginning of the end. It began when the bullets struck President Ronald Reagan in April of that year. Vatican forces through George H.W. Bush and CIA operatives using a Manchurian Candidate, John Hinkley Jr. attempted to assassinate Reagan. Bush was a friend of John Hinkley Sr, who was a CIA asset. They were both in the oil business. Neil Bush, Poppy's oldest son was to have dinner with Hinkley's oldest son the night after the assassination attempt. When the news media got wind of it the dinner was cancelled. So was any further word from the media. The families were obviously close on several levels.

And where was Bush on the day Reagan was shot? In Ft Worth Texas placing some kind of commemorative plaque in the hotel where JFK stayed the night before he was gunned down the next day in Dallas by shooters supervised by Bush and E. Howard Hunt in Dealey Plaza. Really, you can't make this stuff up. They just love the irony don't they? The symbolism. The "in your face" arrogance of being untouchable. But we the people are not stupid. And the truth is on our side. No person on planet earth had a greater motivation to kill Reagan than Bush who was a heartbeat from the presidency. Nor had more intimate knowledge of Reagan's schedule and movements. Nor had a closer relationship with Hinkley. The result was that the US government entered it's final chapter of corruption as a Jesuit controlled beast. A chapter that the prophet Daniel would announce to the whole world as the final installment of corruption. The Reagan assassination attempt was a historical landmark as knowledge of the shadow government began to become public knowledge. And who was at the center of it. It was the beginning of the end for corruption in government, but only the prophet Daniel knew it. The prophecy was sealed. Until now. It would take we the people a bit longer to figure out the timing of his prophecy. Now we know. Now we can look in hindsight and know for certain.

Daniel tells us that 1,290 years from 691AD, in 1981, the beast governments on earth would end. Prophecy dates this divine decree. It is fixed in history. It happened in the year Bush tried to assassinate Reagan. But history teaches us that a date in history, which is certainly confirmed by prophecy fulfilled, is always the beginning of a transition. And the prophet Daniel tells us exactly the same thing because after he announces the 1,290 days "to the end of these wonders" he says . . . "happy are those who come to the 1,335 days!" There it is! Scholars of bible prophecy have puzzled over this for centuries. Why did Daniel add the strange reference to people being happy who "come to the 1,335 years"? Because those who are alive to witness the end of corruption in government are a very blessed and happy generation indeed! We are going to see this! It is us! There is another 45 years we must add to 1981 to see corruption in government end. Or, to witness the coming of righteous government! If we add 45 years to 1981 we come to the year 2026! Just two short years beyond a Trump presidency! Is Donald Trump the man destined to end corruption and pave the way for righteous government? Do you believe the law and prophets of God? Thats the real question. That is the issue really separating people today, splitting the nation wide open. All the rest is just media manipulation. Whose side are you on? Moses asked the same thing.

Prophecy contained in the law and prophets is even so accurate that it alerts us to a specific date within the final 45 year period. Exactly 20 years in, in 2001 on Sept 11th, the "end of days" began! There it is! It is universally declared in all nations that we are in a "post 9-11 world". In other words there is universal recognition that the world changed on that date. And the only people who continue to deny that Sept 11th was a government conspiracy are the media, and those politicians who are afraid to speak out. Those who fear for their lives. Robert Kennedy, another Bush-CIA victim said this: "Few are willing to brave the censure of their colleagues, the wrath of their society. Moral courage is a rarer commodity than bravery in battle, or great intelligence. Yet it is the one essential quality necessary to change a world that yields so painfully to change. And I believe those with the courage to enter the moral conflict will find themselves with companions all over the world". People all over the world know the truth. And it is not the people who should fear or tremble, but those for whom condemnation is reserved.

Is it any wonder, as we near the end of this final 45 year period, as we are now deep into the "end of days", that Donald Trump would openly declare intentions of draining the swamp? Is it coincidence that the Internet, during this period, has made knowledge of government corruption widespread among the people of the world for the first time in history? The thing that has not happened to any extent yet, is the indictments that must surely come. For example, it is widely known that George W. Bush went missing for 3 days and nights while campaigning for president in the summer of 2000. It just so happened that it was the same 3 days and nights when John F. Kennedy Jr's plane went missing. Once JFK Jr was presumed dead, the Gore and Bush campaigns were contacted for statements. Gore said he would not campaign over that weekend out of respect for the Kennedy family. When the press sought out the Bush campaign, not only was there no comment, no one would say where Bush was. Of course there was no outcry or outrage from the press. No demanding the truth. Thats not their business.

There are only two questions in a murder case. Motive and alibi. There is wide speculation that JFK Jr knew the truth of his dad's killing, as well as evidence he did, from articles in his magazine "George". The truth of JFK's killing was in a magazine called . . . George? Published by JFK's son? How ironic is that? There was also wide speculation that he intended to seek high political office, even the White House. No one had a greater motive to kill JFK Jr. than George W. Bush. Had JFK Jr raised the issue of his dad's death and connected George H. W. Bush to it, the history of our nation would have changed course that day. And to this day, Bush has never provided an alibi for his whereabouts over the 3 day period of JFK Jr's plane crash and death. Go ahead. Google "Dark Legacy" George W. Bush and the killing of JFK Jr. Go ahead. There is no statute of limitations on murder. Will we finally begin to see indictments? Prophecy says we will. When we the people have had enough. A swamp contains deadly venomous reptiles. And God declared the eventual destruction of the "seed of the serpent" all the way back in the garden. In the oldest prophecy of them all. But what we have perhaps missed is that the "seed of the woman" the people, are to crush the "seed of the serpent". Thats us. We do the work. Mankind. We the people. We must first of all judge ourselves. Only then will our cry for justice be heard. Thats why Donald Trump is from the people. Why he is not from the elite class of world rulers. He is one of us.

We can no longer look away. Be in denial. Think everything will be alright. Justice is not an inherited birthright. It must be purchased by people often at great cost to themselves. When will a courageous journalist finally break silence? When will a famous media personality break script and shock prime time America? When will a brave filmmaker say, yeah, this is a story we need to tell everyone. How father killed father, and son killed son. Old people in assisted living centers who cherish their remaining years need the truth. Young people in middle schools full of hopes and dreams for the future need the truth. This is our country. It belongs to us. Our national redemption is in our hands. When will one single college or university professor stand before a class and say, "there is a story you need to hear". It is our history, and affects our destiny. How about a little education for a change? When will a pastor, rabbi, cleric or priest finally say, "Enough of religion, we need to tell the truth?!!"

Are we going to leave it all up to Donald Trump? Hope he can somehow overcome generations of institutional corruption? The books written on Bush-Clinton-Jesuit corruption would fill a library. The evidence for Sept 11th is simply overwhelming. We are at a moment of truth unlike any before in our nation's history. We all will be judged. But more than anything, we need to judge ourselves. It is called repentance, turning to do the right thing. That will be the power in our cry, and our work, to bring about justice in this nation. This justice is the door to the Kingdom of God.

Listen to this strange prophecy, speaking of our national well being, written into our own Declaration of Independence: "That whenever any form of government becomes destructive of these ends, it is the right of the people to alter or abolish it, and to institute new government, laying its foundation on such principals and organizing its powers in such a form as to them shall seem most likely to effect their safety and happiness. Prudence indeed will dictate that governments long established should not be changed for light and transient causes, and accordingly all experience hath shown that mankind are more disposed to suffer, while evils are sufferable than to right themselves by abolishing the forms to which they are accustomed. (People will continue to suffer because it is what they know and change is just too daunting.) But when a long train of abuses and usurpations, pursuing invariably the same object evinces a design to reduce them under absolute despotism, it is their right, it is their duty to throw off such government, and to provide new guards for their future security".

Our founders were denouncing the tyranny of the Vatican/British Crown. The Act of 1871 put us right back under it. The Federal Reserve-Vatican-Bank-Of-England-Act of 1913 sealed the deal. It is time to end tyranny, slavery, creeping Socialism, corruption, and Vatican control in America once and for all.

And speaking of Vatican control in America, two Italian writers, speaking for Pope Francis himself, have announced not only Rome's control of America, but of the church in America, as well. Think thats an overstatement? Read on. In a recent July 13 article in the Italian publication, "La Civilta Cattolica" the two Italian writers, Editor Antonia Spadaro, a Jesuit, and Protestant Theologian Marcelo Figueroa, clearly affirm that the

Pope is the sworn enemy of Donald Trump. Our president. Remember, the order to take down JFK originated in the Vatican. Donald Trump has the potential of taking America from the Vatican, which would take down the Vatican itself. He has aroused and shaken the seat of world power to the core. His election was not political. It was prophetic.

And this article proves it. These two writers are very close to Pope Francis. This publication, "La Civilta Cattolica" is the "unofficial voice" of the Papacy. It cannot go to press without "Holy See" approval. It signals to the world what the Pope's position is, albeit what he cannot declare openly. Listen to this. The article basically equates conservative Evangelical and Catholic Trump supporters to Islamic Jihadists, and accuses them of engaging in an "ecumenism of hate". Thats a curious charge for people sharing the same religion, but of course nothing is too outrageous, nonsensical, or off limits when dealing with those who "hate".   It further accuses these "in-the-flesh-devils" of engaging in a ideology of "apocalyptic geopolitics". That their support for legal immigration, deportation, and the wall, must mean they hate people. And, their opposition to "climate change", a ruse to wreak economic havoc on the United States and impose a police state, means they have no interest in preserving planet earth. So all these Trump people must really, in their hearts, hate mankind. What this really means ultimately is that to hold such positions, these people are not "Christian" at all according to the Pope. Reminds me of the Pope's assault on Trump during the campaign when he stated that Trump himself was not "Christian" because he was for building a wall and dividing people. Thats an interesting position for a man who lives behind massive Vatican walls and the most intense security force on the planet. Apparently only his security is of concern.

So, according to the article, its now "Identity Politics" the saviour of mankind, against Trump-"Apocalyptic Geo-politics" which is out to destroy mankind. And, according to the Pope and his writers, conservative Trump supporters, both Protestant and Catholic, are nothing but Islamic Jihadists dressed up like good church goers. Haters, out to kill the unbelievers. The deeper message is that Trump has fueled a kind of "falling away" from eternal truth, with this embracing of hate that unites conservatives in both arms of the Pope's church. Here is the answer to that. You can't fall away from a lie. You can realize you have been lied to. And leave.

This article on the Pope's position affirms the truth of TRUMPROPHECY, and the magnitude of what we are dealing with. For the hundreds of millions of sincere Protestant and Catholic Christian believers, not only in America but all over the world, who love God, and who only want the truth, the leader of your religion doesn't give a damn about what you really believe. Or about you. He only wants to control you. And your nation. He is the hater, and its now Inquisition III. But not much longer. One day, and very soon, hundreds of millions will flee this man and his covenant with death, his agreement with hell. When that day comes freedom will cry at last, from every nation in this world.

That cry, freedom's cry, has begun in America. Trump's recent visit to the Vatican in May was characterized by all as "chilly" with the Supreme Pontiff lacking his usual "warmth and cheerfulness". The cry for freedom has begun.

An here is perhaps the deepest irony of all. Please think about this. The Pope and his writers, with this article, are accelerating a strategic campaign to undermine church support for Trump in America, and really what he stands for around the world. They are part of the coup to take him down. Think about it. They are now defining a "Christian" (according to the Church in Rome) by their political convictions. If those convictions don't line up with Church doctrine, church authority, then you are really not "Christian" at all. You are just one who "hates". Somewhere between the KKK and the Islamic Jihadists. Sound familiar? Kind of a "politically correct" Inquisition. They can't burn you at the stake exactly, or gas you and shove you into the ovens, but they can make your life a politically correct hell. A living nightmare. They can help install the Obamas and Bush-Clintons and Bernie Sanders of the world to run your government, and ruin your life.

So lets just put it out there. This is for the hundreds of millions of Protestant and Catholic believers all over the world. I was one of you for 35 years before I learned the truth. If your conscience, your instincts, indeed your heart is telling you Trump is doing the right thing, but your church is attempting to dictate something politically correct, and define that as "Christian" then are YOU really . . . "Christian"? Or have you been seduced and lied to? If you love God and want only the truth, then maybe you are an Old Testament person of God, and your heart is seeking the Covenant of God. Deep calleth unto deep. And the liberty of conscience that God gave you to discern between right and wrong is causing you to respond to Trump taking on a corrupt world system. You know in your heart that something is radically wrong in this world. So it is not politics, but truth you are responding to. It is God speaking to your heart through Trump. Bypassing the theology and political ideology of Rome. God is truth, but truth. . . is also God. If a man shall do right, shall he not live? Isn't that true repentance? When we turn from what is wrong and attempt to do that which is right? Isn't that what Trump is doing?

Trump is attempting to lay the foundation for a new government. The Roman Empire is finally coming to an end. Forever. And here is where we must lay the foundation for our new government: In the Law of God. It must be the foundation of our principals, and upon which we must organize our powers. You see, the Western Democracies are often conflated with Christianity. They are based, not on Christianity, but on the Law of God, the Ten Commandments. That is why they have enjoyed the only relative freedom the world has ever known. Christianity teaches that the Law of God has been done away with. That it is null and void. It also obliterates what the prophets actually revealed about the Kingdom Of God. It destroys both pillars upon which the truth stands. This actually undermines Western Civilization.

The entire foundation of English and American Common Law is the eternal

Covenant God gave to the Joseph people. The Law of Moses. It teaches that man is sovereign with unalienable rights coming directly from God, but, demands a corresponding responsibility to the law, on the part of people. Socialism is the sworn enemy of the Law of God. All rights are conferred by the state, a counterfeit "God" with puppet rulers who can then deny those rights. So legally, they are not rights at all, but merely state permissions, requiring a license or state ordered qualification. God's rights to an individual are unalienable. One cannot be separated from them. It is the ultimate defense to tyranny and dictatorship. It carries with it a high personal responsibility to family, to community, and to the nation. Righteousness is doing the right thing. The fruit of righteousness, is peace.

JFK saw this not just as an American issue, but as an issue affecting all mankind in every nation. Listen to what he said upon taking the Oath of Office: "I have sworn before you, and Almighty God the same solemn oath, our forbears prescribed nearly a century and three quarters ago. And yet the same, revolutionary beliefs, for which our forbears fought, are still at issue around the globe. The belief that the rights of man come not from the generosity of the state, but from the hand of God. We dare not forget today, that we are the heirs of that first revolution. . ." He was warning this nation and indeed the world, that we as a people must not forget the Law of God upon which our liberty, sovereignty, and rights depend. Or we will repeat the tragedy of nations who do. That we, in our time, in this nation, must "Remember the Law of Moses". We must turn to it now, or sink into the abyss of dictatorship the likes of which the world has never seen.

This is where TRUMPROPHECY reaches it's most stunning and fascinating conclusion. The Law of God has actually moved into the White House. Jarad and Ivanka are obeying the Law of God, while operating as the two closest and most trusted advisors to President Trump. They represent the link now between Joseph and Judah. Ivanka is from the House of Joseph and Jarad is from the House of Judah. Prophecy tells us when this repair of the breach happens, between Joseph and Judah, the entire re-united House of Joseph will return to the Law of God and order their national life accordingly. It will be America's national redemption, her finest hour, and door to the Kingdom of God.

Jarad and Ivanka are Sabbath Keepers. They are in Covenant with God. This is why they both are increasingly savaged, mocked, criticized and attacked. President Trump is an Old Testament man of God. He is not of the Church, and it is very obvious. He is seeking to do the right thing. That will bring righteousness and peace upon our nation. Donald Trump is the greatest friend the orthodox, covenant keeping House of Judah has ever had in the White House. His own family represents the repair of the breach between Joseph and Judah! The leadership in Israel is 100% behind our president. Not only that, he is a builder. Perhaps the greatest in the world. Who better to build a new temple, to house a new government, based on the Law of God?

He is operating to bring about true justice in an atmosphere of injustice and corruption and media manipulation. He is piercing the great national lie, with the truth. He is actually attempting to bring about righteousness in government. This national ref-ormation can only lead to the downfall of this final government of Rome seen by the prophet so long ago.

The hour is fast approaching. When it happens we will all be home at last. We can dance in the streets. Praise and thanks to our great God for a man many of us have waited and prayed for. Donald J. Trump, 45th President Of The United States.

God speed Mr. President. Take us home.

. . . and Yahweh has vowed to you America, this day, to be his special people, as he has promised you, that you should keep all his commandments, and to make you high above all nations which he has made, in praise, in honor, in beauty, that you may be a holy people unto the Lord your God, as he has spoken . . .

The Beginning . . .

This writing was written over an intense 8 week period. It was 40 years in the making.
Thank you for reading, or listening to it. Don Rohrer

7th and Final Edit - August 21st 2017